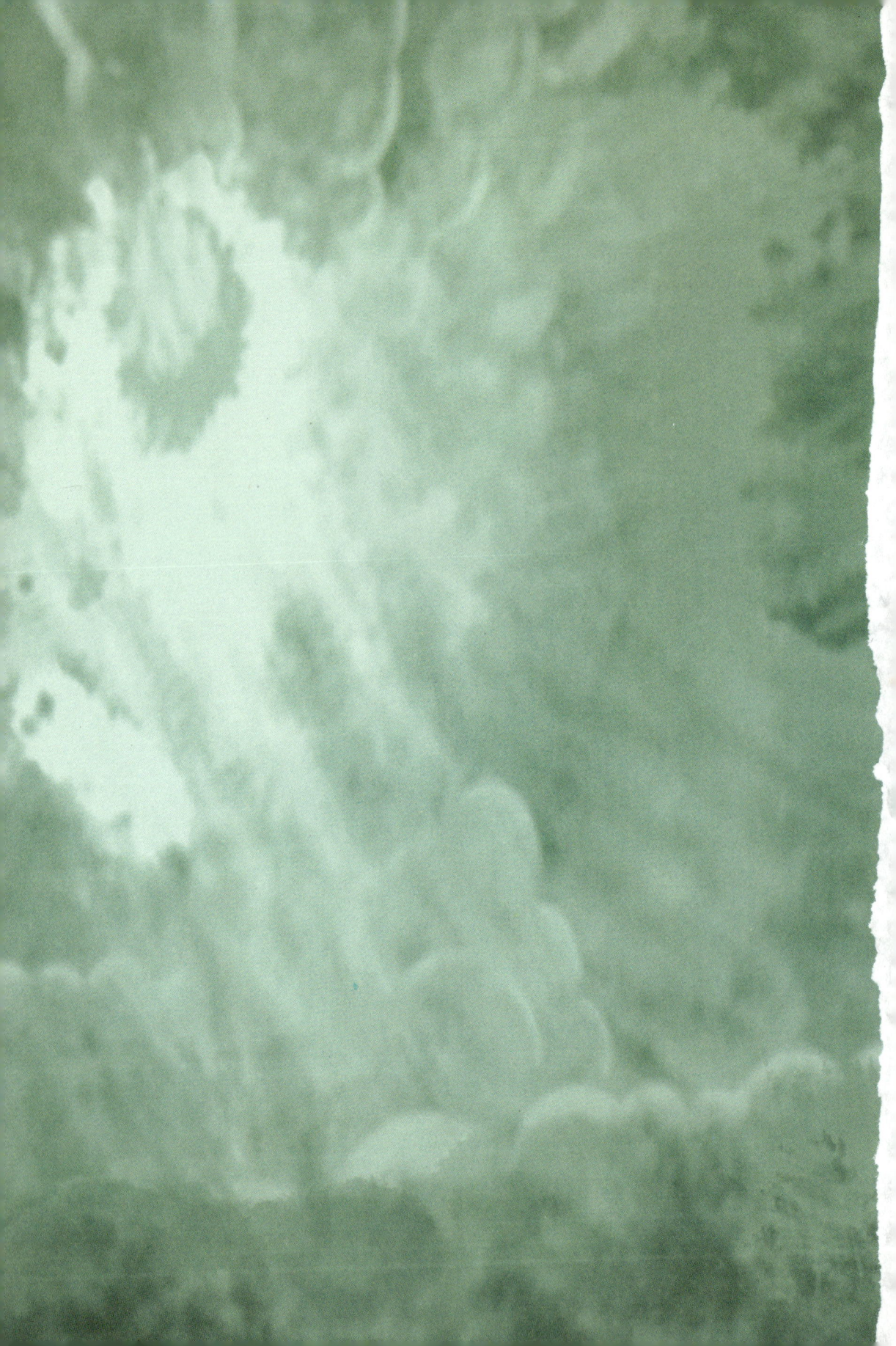

Ramayana
for children

Sudha Gupta

www.pegasusforkids.com

© **B. Jain Publishers (P) Ltd.** All rights reserved. No part of this book may be reproduced, stored in a retrieval system or transmitted, in any form or by any means, mechanical, photocopying, recording or otherwise, without any prior written permission of the publisher.

Published by Kuldeep Jain for B. Jain Publishers (P) Ltd., D-157, Sector 63, Noida - 201307, U.P.
Registered office: 1921/10, Chuna Mandi, Paharganj, New Delhi-110055
Printed in India

Contents

The Birth of Rama 5
Sage Vishwamitra's Arrival 11
Rama Slays Demons 14
Mareecha and Subahu 18
The Story of Ahalya 22
Rama Weds Sita 26
Meeting Parashurama 30
Rama Chosen to be Yuvraja 34
Manthara's Evil Plan 37
Kaikeyi's Demands 42
Rama's Banishment 48
Sita's Resolve 52
Off to the Forest 56
The Story of Shravan Kumar 61
Dasharatha's Last Moments 64
Bharata Returns 66
Intrigue Wasted 68
The Brothers Meet 74
Off to Panchavati 80
Soorpanakha's Proposal 84
Khara and Dushana are Killed 88
The Path of Ruin 90
The Golden Deer 92
Sita's Abduction 94
Brave Jatayu 96

In Search of Sita	97
Shabari's Berries	101
Rama Sugriva Alliance	104
The Slaying of Vali	112
The Search Begins	116
Sampati Helps	120
The Son of Vayu	123
A Fascinating Leap	124
Hanuman Reaches Lanka	128
Ashoka Vatika	131
Hanuman Meets Sita	134
Hanuman is Captured	136
Lanka on Fire	138
Good Tidings Conveyed	141
Vibhishana Meets Rama	144
Crossing the Sea	148
The Battle Begins	152
Serpent Darts	154
The Giant is Roused	157
Sanjeevani Booti	160
The Slaying of Indrajit	164
End of Ravana	166
The Test of Fire	173
Rama the King of Ayodhya	184
Birth of Luv and Kush	187
Sita Enters the Earth	190
Last Days of Rama	192

The Birth of Rama

On the north of River Ganga was situated the great kingdom of Kosala, in the present day Uttar Pradesh. River Sarayu ran through the kingdom, making it fertile. Its capital city was Ayodhya, built by Manu, the greatest leader of the Solar Dynasty and the first ruler of mankind. After Manu, Surya Vansha or the Solar Dynasty lineage witnessed some of the greatest kings such as Harishchandra, Sagar, Asmanjan, Anshuman, Bhagiratha, Dileep, Raghu, Aja and Dasharatha. King Dasharatha ruled the kingdom from the capital city of Ayodhya. Surrounded by the best ministers, with Sumantra as chief counsellor, and guided by the royal priests such as Vashishtha, King Dasharatha's splendour shone as the rising sun.

In the midst of all this prosperity, Dasharatha remained sad, as he had no heir. His grief was not hidden from his council of ministers.

One day, Sumantra suggested to the king, "Maharaja, why don't you perform a Putra-prapti Yajna?" Sumantra further added that Sage Rishyasringa should be invited to perform the yajna to which Dasharatha agreed.

Soon the preparations for the yajna began. The yajna was a grand affair with invitees being the great kings of the neighbouring kingdoms. Sage Rishyasringa began the yajna by lighting the holy fire, and soon the entire place resounded with the chanting of sacred Vedic mantras.

Meanwhile, the gods in heaven discussed about a growing threat of that time. Together, all the gods went to Lord Brahma, the creator, to complain about Ravana, the king of demons. With the boon granted by Lord Brahma, Ravana was invincible against devas, asuras and gandharvas. With this boon, he planned to overthrow the gods from heaven too.

"You must stop him," the gods pleaded to Lord Brahma.

Brahma was aware that though Ravana was invincible against devas, asuras and gandharvas, but he lacked invincibility against humans.

As Lord Brahma pondered over the problem, he looked down and saw Dasharatha's yajna in progress. At that moment, he decided to ask Lord Vishnu, the preserver of the universe, to be born on earth in human form.

Led by Lord Brahma, all the gods requested Lord Vishnu to be born on earth as Dasharatha's son, to kill Ravana. Vishnu agreed, and at the same moment, the yajna fire started to glow brighter.

As the ghee was poured into the fire and the flames shot up, a majestic figure appeared from the flames. He was holding a golden bowl.

To King Dasharatha, the figure said, "The devas are pleased with you. This divine payasam has been sent by them for your wives. Give it to them and you will be blessed with sons soon."

With unbounded joy, Dasharatha received the bowl and distributed the payasam (rice pudding) among his three wives, Kaushalya, Sumitra and Kaikeyi. Kaushalya drank half of the payasam. Sumitra drank half of what remained. Half of what was then left was drunk by Kaikeyi and what remained was given to Sumitra again.

In due course of time, Dasharatha was blessed with four sons: Rama of Kaushalya, Bharata of Kaikeyi, and Sumitra gave birth to twins, Lakshmana and Shatrughna as she had drunk the divine payasam twice.

Dasharatha was glad to see his four sons grow up strong, virtuous, brave and lovable, and with all other princely qualities. Rama and Lakshmana were especially devoted to each other and so were Bharata and Shatrughna to one another.

Sage Vishwamitra's Arrival

One day, as King Dasharatha sat in his court, a messenger came in to announce the arrival of Sage Vishwamitra. Sage Vishwamitra was respected for his vast knowledge and divine perception. But he was feared for his bad temper.

King Dasharatha welcomed the sage. With great reverence, the king said, "I am blessed by your presence. Is there anything that I can do for you? Please command and I shall obey."

Vishwamitra said, "I am engaged in performing a sacrifice. As it nears completion, two powerful demons Mareecha and Subahu, defile it constantly. They shower unclean blood and flesh on the sacred fire. Our troubles can end if you send your brave sons Rama and Lakshmana with me to kill these powerful demons."

Hearing this, Dasharatha grew anxious. He shuddered to think of sending the young princes amongst the dreadful demons. He said to the sage, "My sons are so young. How can they fight demons I will give you my army instead."

Dasharatha's attempt to go back on his words enraged Vishwamitra. "This conduct is unworthy of your lineage!" the sage said. "If this is your final word, I shall go back the way I came!"

At this moment, Sage Vashishtha intervened and spoke gently, "O King, send Rama and Lakshmana with the sage. You don't have to fear about their safety when they are protected by Sage Vishwamitra. Do not hesitate."

On Sage Vashishtha's advice, Dasharatha agreed to send Rama and Lakshmana. With the blessings of their father, mothers and Sage Vashishtha, the princes prepared for their journey.

Rama Slays Demons

At the crack of dawn, the two princes started their journey with Sage Vishwamitra. Crossing River Ganga, Vishwamitra and the princes made their way through a dense forest.

Looking around, Vishwamitra said, "This is the Dandaka forest. Once upon a time, men, animals, birds and insects lived happily here. But this was until Tadaka wreaked havoc and changed this into the dreadful wilderness it has now become."

Vishwamitra pointed to a cave at a distant hill and said, "Tadaka lives in that cave. She is capable of smelling human flesh from afar. I want you to draw her out of the cave and kill her."

On the orders of the sage, Rama strung his bow and twanged it till the forest echoed its shrill note.

Tadaka, who was sleeping in her cave, woke up on hearing the sound. "Who dares to enter my forest?" she screamed.

Raging with anger, she came out and ran in the direction from where the sound had come.

Like all demons, Tadaka too had magical powers. Rising in the sky, she rained stones on Rama and Lakshmana. The two princes defended very well and a ferocious battle ensued. The fight continued with evening approaching.

Sage Vishwamitra cautioned Rama, saying, "The sun is about to set. Remember, at night demons grow stronger. Do not delay in slaying her!"

Thus advised, Rama took out a deadly arrow and aimed at Tadaka. The arrow pierced her chest, and the huge, ugly monster fell down, lifeless. The moment Tadaka died, birds started chirping, plants began to flower, and trees started to bear fruits. A pleased Vishwamitra blessed Rama, and gifted him some of the most powerful weapons such as Dandachakra, Kaalchakra, and Brahmastra.

Mareecha and Subahu

Rama and Lakshmana continued their journey with Sage Vishwamitra. In due course of their journey, they reached Siddhashrama which was Vishwamitra's hermitage. After they settled down, Sage Vishwamitra began the preparations for the yajna. The next morning, Vishwamitra, along with his disciples, started the yajna, which was to be performed for six days and nights. The princes kept vigil throughout that time.

On the morning of the sixth day, Rama said to Lakshmana, "Brother, now is the time for the enemies to come. Let us remain alert."

The next moment, they heard a great roar in the sky and two giants appeared. They were Tadaka's sons Mareecha and Subahu.

Rama looked up and saw Mareecha and Subahu preparing to defile the yajna by showering unclean things. As Mareecha charged towards them, the two princes stood unmoved with their minds working rapidly. They were aware that even hundreds of ordinary arrows were not enough to kill a powerful demon like Mareecha.

Rama started chanting the mantra to invoke the divine weapons, as taught to them by Sage Vishwamitra. Thunder roared, lightning flashed, as Manavastra went flying towards Mareecha. He was flung far away to the bottom of the deep sea.

Next, Rama invoked another divine weapon called Agneyastra, created by Agni, god of fire. Rama aimed this divine weapon at Subahu. It hit him, and within moments, he was just a heap of ashes on the ground.

All the sages thanked Rama and Lakshmana, and blessed them for bringing peace to the ashrama.

The Story of Ahalya

The next day, Vishwamitra accompanied by Rama and Lakshmana, started his journey towards Mithila. Here, King Janaka was holding a swayamvara for his daughter Sita.

On the way, they saw a beautiful ashrama which looked quite desolate. Rama asked Vishwamitra, "Whose ashrama is this with such ancient trees? Why does such a beautiful abode stand deserted?"

Vishwamitra replied, "This is the ashrama of Sage Gautama. Years ago, he lived here peacefully with his wife Ahalya. One day, when he was away, Indra, the king of gods, came to the ashrama disguised as Gautama. He flattered Ahalya with so much attention that

she had no reason to believe that he was an imposter and not her husband. However, as fate would have it, Sage Gautama returned unexpectedly. On seeing Indra in disguise, he was enraged. He was also enraged by his wife's lack of faithfulness.

Angrily, he cursed her, "This beauty of yours, which has made you so vain, will turn into a cold piece of rock. You shall turn to stone!"

The moment Sage Gautama said these words, Ahalya turned into stone. Moments later, when his anger vanished, Sage Gautama realised that his wife was not at fault. However, he could not take his curse back. So he said, "When Rama, the son of Ayodhya's King Dasharatha, will visit this place, you will regain your original beauty and form."

"Let us enter the ashrama. You will bring redemption to Ahalya and rekindle the light in her as the sage promised," said Vishwamitra to Rama.

So they stepped inside the ashrama. Moved by compassion, Rama stepped forward and touched the stone statue of the beautiful Ahalya. The next moment, the stone figure transformed into a human form, and Ahalya came to life.

Rama and Lakshmana touched the feet of the sage's wife made pure by penance. Ahalya welcomed the princes to the ashrama. At this moment, Sage Gautama also returned to the ashrama and welcomed Ahalya back as his wife once again.

Rama Weds Sita

After spending the night at Sage Gautama's ashrama Rama and Lakshmana resumed their journey towards Mithila.

King Janaka of Mithila had a daughter named Sita, who was destined to marry Lord Vishnu in human form. She had reached the marriageable age, but Janaka was unable to find a prince worthy of Sita. Hence, he decided to hold a swayamvara for his daughter.

All arrangements had been completed and princes from various kingdoms had come to Mithila to attend the swayamvara. Vishwamitra and the princes of Ayodhya were also duly welcomed.

King Janaka proclaimed, "Sita, my daughter, will be given in marriage to the prince who can lift, bend and string the bow of Shiva, which Varuna gave me and to none other!"

Moments later, the famous bow was brought to the venue. Kings and princes from all the neighbouring kingdoms came decked in jewels and in the finest of silk attire. They were seated surrounding the bow, which was kept on a huge eight-wheeled cart.

One by one, all the kings and princes came up to pick up the bow. However, not a single one could even move it from its place.

Then, after obtaining permission from Vishwamitra and King Janaka, Rama stepped forward to lift the bow. The next moment, he lifted the bow effortlessly. As he bent to string the bow and drew the string back, the mighty bow snapped with a crash.

The quietness was broken by the sounds of drums and conchs, with flowers being showered from heaven above. King Janaka proclaimed, "My beloved daughter shall be wedded to this young man."

Sita wedded Rama by placing a garland around his neck.

Vishwamitra told Janaka, "Send your messengers to Ayodhya to give the news to King Dasharatha."

Dasharatha was filled with joy on hearing the good news. Immediately, he started his journey towards Mithila, accompanied by his wives.

King Janaka's brother Kushadhwaja was the king of Sankasya. He

was blessed with two charming and beautiful daughters called Mandavi and Shrutkirti. The two sages, Vashishtha and Vishwamitra proposed that Mandavi and Shrutkirti be married to Bharata and Shatrughna respectively. They also proposed that for Lakshmana, Sita's younger sister Urmila was a worthy match. Thus, at the same altar, the four brothers were married.

With Rama and Sita joined in an eternal bond, Mithila was like a heavenly city with unending celebrations for ten days.

Meeting Parashurama

After seeking Janaka's blessings, Sita and her sisters took leave to start their journey towards their new home, Ayodhya. The procession was enroute to Ayodhya when their path was blocked by an eminent sage called Parashurama.

Though born as a brahmin, Parashurama was one of the fiercest warriors. His love for and knowledge of all divine weapons, and his hatred towards the kshatriyas or the warrior class, set him apart from

the other sages. Known to be Vishnu incarnate for the sixth time, he stood there blocking the path, holding an axe in his hands.

"The thunderous sound of the snapping of Pinaka has drawn me here. Shiva's great bow has been broken," said Parashurama.

Then looking at Rama, he said, "Son of Dasharatha, I have heard of your prowess. Here is my bow, equal in all respects to the one that you broke. This is the bow of Vishnu which was entrusted to my father. Take it and let all of us see if you can place an arrow on it after stringing it."

Rama bowed and gladly took the bow. With casual ease, he uncoiled the string from around the bow, strung it and knocked an arrow. Parashurama's face fell as he realised that it was indeed Vishnu, of whom he himself was a part, who stood in front of him.

Rama still had the arrow knocked to the bow.

"O great sage, the arrow once knocked to the great bow of Vishnu, must be directed towards a target. I can't commit the sin of slaying a brahmin. Hence, I must either destroy the merit you have earned through your severe penances or your power of locomotion at mind's speed. Which will it be?" asked Rama.

To this, Parashurama replied with a smile, "Pray, do not rid me of my powers of locomotion, which I need to traverse back to my abode in Mahendra Mountain, for I am forbidden to spend even a day on earth by Kashyapa. Destroy, instead, the merits of my penance."

Rama chanted divine mantras that converted the arrow into a beam of light which he aimed at the sage. Parashurama's wish was fulfilled. He lost all his spiritual powers and piety gained through severe penance. With this, Parashurama took their leave and disappeared.

Thereafter, Rama and family made its way back to Ayodhya, where the couples were welcomed with great love and enthusiasm.

Rama Chosen to be Yuvraja

Rama and Sita lived happily in Ayodhya for twelve years. Though Dasharatha loved all his sons, yet he had a special affection for Rama. Rama's virile beauty, his strength and courage, the purity of his heart, his deep wisdom and his statesmanship were admired by the people of Ayodhya. They eagerly looked forward to Rama becoming their king.

Growing old, Dasharatha decided to hand over the reins of his empire to Rama and coronate him as the crown prince. With this thought, he

convened a meeting of his ministers. "Like my ancestors, I have tended this kingdom as a mother cares for her child. I have worked tirelessly for the people. Now my body is old and infirm. I wish, therefore, to appoint my eldest son as Yuvraja and transfer to him the burden of my responsibilities."

Shouts of joyous acclaim rose from the assembly and all affirmed, "So be it!"

Hearing the decision to anoint him Yuvraja, Rama humbly bowed in acceptance, saying, "I am duty bound to carry out your orders, whatever they may be."

Sage Vashishtha suggested that the coronation should be performed the next day itself, as it was an auspicious day in the month of Chaitra. To this, King Dasharatha agreed.

Alas! If only the king knew that fate had something else in store!

Although Rama was an incarnation of Lord Vishnu himself, he too had to undergo the pain and suffering of an ordinary mortal. While under the harsh realities of life, an ordinary man would have broken down, Rama never wavered from his duties as a human being. Rightfully, therefore, he is called Maryada Purushottam, one who would never waver from the path of righteous deeds.

Manthara's Evil Plan

Once the royal decision was taken, the news spread like wildfire. The three queens Kaushalya, Sumitra and Kaikeyi were overjoyed to hear this news. Kaushalya blessed her son, "May you live long. Be a good ruler. Conquer your foes and protect your subjects and kinsfolk."

The city of Ayodhya was immersed in celebrations once again. Houses were decorated with flowers, festoons and flags. The city was in a joyous commotion of expectancy. The people of Ayodhya looked at the coronation as a great and auspicious occasion in their lives and looked forward to it with enthusiasm.

Lakshmana was at Rama's side throughout. However, Bharata and Shatrughna were away during this time, visiting Kaikeyi's parents.

As everyone in the city of Ayodhya rejoiced and prepared for the coronation of Rama, an old woman watched everything quietly from the window of Kaikeyi's palace. She was Manthara, a hunchback, Queen Kaikeyi's maid for past many years. Being a distant relative of the queen's family, she claimed great intimacy with her.

Unable to restrain her thoughts, and filled with anger, Manthara entered Kaikeyi's chamber and called out to her, "O foolish queen, how can you be blind to the misfortune that is approaching you? Dasharatha has decided to make Rama the ruler of this land. With this, Kaushalya, who has always been jealous of you, will rise to power and fame."

Shocked with Manthara's sudden outburst of anger, Kaikeyi said, "Manthara, I am aware of all the developments at Ayodhya. But don't forget, Rama is my son too. Today, it is the day of celebration. Here, take this pearl necklace. I am so happy today!"

With this, she threw the necklace towards Manthara. This increased Manthara's grief. She flung the necklace to the ground and said, "You are a fool! From tomorrow your son Bharata will be a slave to Rama. Would not Rama then look upon Bharata as a dangerous enemy? Hereafter, Bharata's life is in danger."

Hearing these words from Manthara, the queen stopped doing everything and sat down to listen intently. Manthara was happy to see that she was successful in capturing Kaikeyi's full attention.

"What are you talking about?" asked Kaikeyi.

Thus, Manthara spoke, filled with vehemence, "O dear queen, I always knew that you were as innocent as a dove. Can't you foresee the impending danger if Rama becomes the Yuvraja? Didn't you find it strange that King Dasharatha announced Rama's coronation at a time when Bharata is away? If there was no evil intention, then the king would have at least consulted you before taking the royal decision. Kaushalya was consulted and the decision was made. O queen, what more proof do you need of your declining status in the palace?"

Fear now entered the heart of Queen Kaikeyi. Helpless, she clung to Manthara for comfort and safety, "What shall I do, Manthara? I am scared!"

Manthara had successfully poisoned the queen's mind. She started in a soft voice, "This is indeed strange! Have you really forgotten?

Or, are you pretending? Do you remember how your husband Dasharatha, long ago, got wounded in a battle and fell unconscious? Then, you drove his chariot skillfully out of the battlefield, gently removed the arrows from his body and saved his life. Remember, when he recovered, he granted you two boons. And you had said that I don't need anything now. I will ask whenever I need. The time has arrived to ask for your two boons from the king. As your first wish, demand that Bharata should be crowned instead of Rama. And as second wish, ask him to banish Rama from Ayodhya and send him for fourteen years of exile."

Manthara further said, "Do as I tell you. Throw away your fine robes and your jewels, wear old clothes and lie down on the floor. Do not yield on any terms when the king visits you. Insist on the two boons."

Kaikeyi's Demands

After dismissing the assembly and giving orders for the preparations and celebrations of the coronation ceremony, Dasharatha sought the company of his favourite wife to share his happiness and excitement. He went to Queen Kaikeyi's chamber.

The place bore an unusually sombre look. On asking for the reason, the attendants said, folding their hands in reverence, "Lord, the queen is angry."

The moment Dasharatha entered the room, he saw a sight that amazed and distressed him. Kaikeyi lay on the bare floor in old robes and with disheveled hair, like one in mortal pain.

Dasharatha knelt beside her and asked her fondly, "O queen, what has come over you? Are you not well?"

Kaikeyi sighed heavily, but would not speak.

Dasharatha continued, "O dear, please speak! Have you received any bad news? Please tell me. My heart breaks to see you in such a state."

Kaikeyi paid no attention to his questions and remained silent. At last the king said, "State your wish. It shall be done. Ask me anything and it shall be granted at once!"

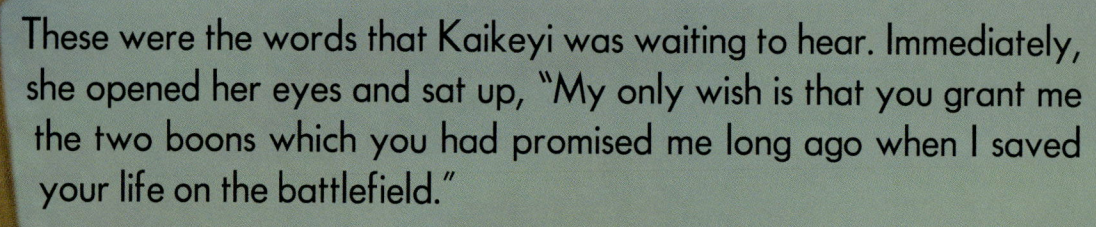

These were the words that Kaikeyi was waiting to hear. Immediately, she opened her eyes and sat up, "My only wish is that you grant me the two boons which you had promised me long ago when I saved your life on the battlefield."

The king nodded in agreement, recalling the incident years back and the promise he had made.

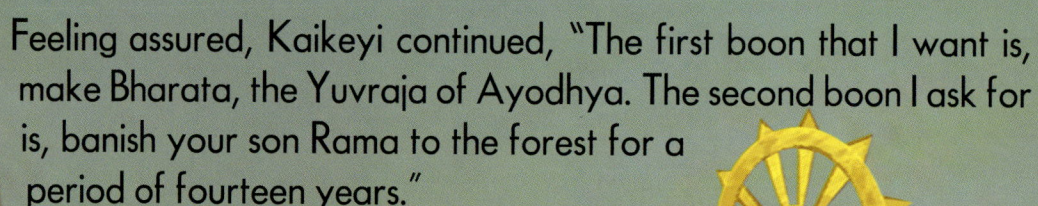

Feeling assured, Kaikeyi continued, "The first boon that I want is, make Bharata, the Yuvraja of Ayodhya. The second boon I ask for is, banish your son Rama to the forest for a period of fourteen years."

Dasharatha was thunder-struck! He couldn't believe what he had just heard.

"Could it be other than a nightmare? I am certainly the victim of an illusion!" With these words, he fainted. After some time, when he regained consciousness, he said, "O wicked queen, what harm has Rama done to you? Has he not looked upon you as his own mother?"

Kaikeyi was unmoved and didn't speak a word.

The king continued, "Who has poisoned your mind? I cannot believe that this evil thought is your own. How often have you told me, my dear, that, noble as Bharata is, Rama is nobler still? Is it the same Rama that you now want to be exiled to the forest?"

Blinded by greed, jealousy and treachery, Kaikeyi remained unmoved.

"O Kaikeyi, ask for anything else in this kingdom, and I will give. I beg you humbly, save Rama! Save me from sin!" To the king thus struggling in a sea of grief, pitiless Kaikeyi said, "You promised me two boons and at this hour of time, I want them.

What sort of king would you be if you don't follow your dharma?"

Manthara watched all this, hidden in a corner, and felt jubilant. Dasharatha, completely heartbroken, agreed to grant Kaikeyi's two boons. Thus, he consented on making Bharata the Yuvraja and banishing Rama to the forest.

Rama's Banishment

Grief-stricken King Dasharatha resigned himself to his fate. The day dawned, and the hour for coronation was fast approaching. The procession of sages led by Sage Vashishtha carrying the golden vessels containing the waters of holy rivers, was fast approaching the palace gates.

At that moment, Kaikeyi called the messenger and said, "King Dasharatha wants to meet Rama before coronation. Go at once and give the message to him."

On getting the message, Rama rushed to Kaikeyi's chamber As he stepped inside the room, he was shocked to see his father lying on the bare floor in anguish. Rama was filled with apprehension at the sight of his father, lying there unable to speak, in the grip of some great agony. What could it be, Rama could never guess!

Looking at Kaikeyi, he said, "O mother, what is the cause of his worry? Is my father angry with me?"

Kaikeyi spoke thus, "The king is angry with no one. However, he is afraid to share with you what is in his mind. Once upon a time, pleased with me, he offered me a gift of two boons, which I accepted. Now, the king regrets he did so. You have the power to fulfil his promise, but he fears even to tell you of it."

Rama was sad to know that he was the cause of his father's distress. He said to Kaikeyi, "Mother, I give you my solemn promise that I shall fulfil my father's promise to you. And I never break my word!"

Thereupon, the pitiless Kaikeyi uttered these terrible words, "Rama, your words are worthy of you. What higher duty has a son than helping fulfilment of the word his father has given? Here is what I want as my two boons: Bharata should be anointed as Yuvraja and you should be exiled to the forest for a period of fourteen years starting from this very day."

Contrary to Kaikeyi's expectation, rather than appearing shocked, Rama looked as calm as before, "Mother, I know that you will never think anything bad for me. Your word is my command. Would I not be happy to give anything to Bharata? Even if no one asked me, I would cheerfully give him my all. I shall go to the forest this very day, with no regrets. Kindly take care of my father and tell him not to worry for me."

Rama took leave of his father and Kaikeyi, and proceeded to his own mother Kaushalya's chamber to seek her blessings. Lakshmana had been standing outside the chamber and had heard everything. With eyes filled with tears, he followed Rama.

Sita's Resolve

Rama, accompanied by Lakshmana, went to Kaushalya's chamber. Kaushalya had already heard the news and was inconsolable. As soon as Rama entered, she embraced him, but unable to contain her grief, fell on the ground, unconscious.

Gaining consciousness, she said, "Don't go to the forest. If you go away, how will I stay here alone? I too shall accompany you."

To this plea of Kaushalya, Rama said, "Mother, let there be no talk of anyone going with me to the forest. It is my duty to fulfil my father's word and it is your duty to stay here serving the king and sharing the sorrow that has befallen him in his old age."

Lakshmana could not bear the sight of the queen's grief. Angrily, he spoke, "Instead of the sun rising, a great darkness has descended upon the land this morning. For, when we were expecting your coronation, the king sentences you to banishment! Don't agree to this! If you go to the forest, I will not stay behind too."

Rama consoled Lakshmana by saying, "Our highest duty is to fulfil our father's word and enable him to fulfil his pledge. If we fail in that, no other achievement can make up for it."

However, Rama couldn't make Lakshmana agree on not accompanying him to the forest.

When Sita heard this unexpected news, she rushed to Kaushalya's chamber. She entered when Rama was consoling Lakshmana.

"I, too, will come with you, my Lord," came Sita's voice from the far corner.

Rama tried to convince Sita and tried to dissuade her by accounting the hardships that she would face in the forest.

However, Sita was resolute, "I hold that your fortunes are mine and if you have to go to the forest, the command includes me as well, as I am a part of you. To go with you wherever you go is my only dharma." And thus, it was settled that Rama would be accompanied by Sita and Lakshmana on his fourteen-year exile in the forest.

Off to the Forest

Taking leave of Mother Kaushalya, Rama, accompanied by Sita and Lakshmana, ascended the chariot. Sumantra drove the chariot towards the gates of the kingdom.

Swarms of people gathered on the streets, and cried, addressing the charioteer, "Go slow, go slow! Let us have a look at Rama's face. Alas! Who could send such children to the forest?"

The people of the city followed Rama's chariot, trying to stop it, shouting, "Do not go to the forest! Return to the city!"

Rama stopped the chariot and addressed them, "O citizens of Ayodhya, I know the love you bear for me. You will show it best by transferring it on my behalf, and at my behest, to my beloved brother Bharata. Nothing else will please me more. You and I alike should obey the king's commands. So you should go back home in peace."

However, the people didn't pay heed to what Rama said and continued to follow the chariot. The chariot stopped at the bank of River Tamasa. That night, Rama and Sita slept on the river bank, while Lakshmana kept vigil.

Long before dawn, Rama rose from sleep and said to Sumantra, "The citizens who have followed us are fast asleep. Let us, therefore, move now, before they wake up."

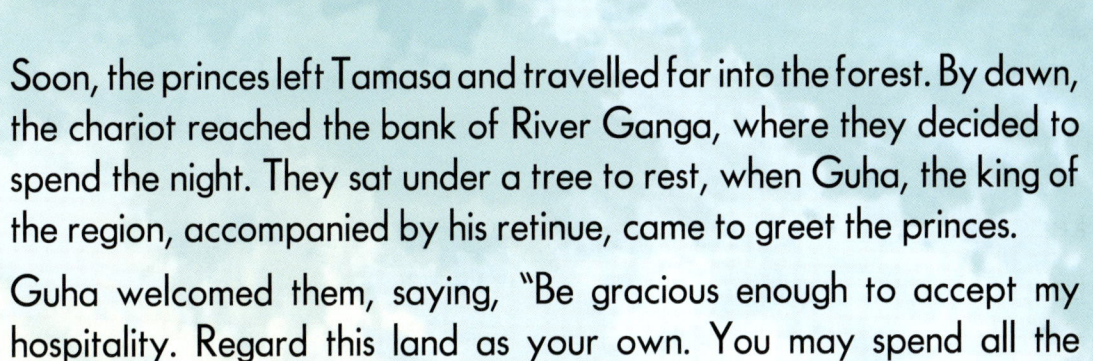

Soon, the princes left Tamasa and travelled far into the forest. By dawn, the chariot reached the bank of River Ganga, where they decided to spend the night. They sat under a tree to rest, when Guha, the king of the region, accompanied by his retinue, came to greet the princes.

Guha welcomed them, saying, "Be gracious enough to accept my hospitality. Regard this land as your own. You may spend all the fourteen years with us here."

To this Rama replied, "Brother, I know how deep is your love for me. I am bound by my vows and must refuse anything more. I would be grateful if you can help us in crossing the river by giving us a boat. We will stay here for the night and proceed in the morning."

The next morning, Sumantra stood seeking further commands from Rama.

Rama understood Sumantra's unuttered grief and said, "Sumantra, return to Ayodhya and be at the side of the king. Your duty is now to look after him."

After bidding farewell to Guha, Rama, Lakshmana and Sita sat in the boat and the boatman rowed it across to the farthest bank of River Ganga. They spent that night at Rishi Bharadwaja's ashrama. The next morning, taking leave of him, they started their journey towards Chitrakuta hill where they planned to build their abode.

The Story of Shravan Kumar

After reaching Ayodhya, without even wasting a moment, Sumantra rushed to King Dasharatha's chamber. There he saw the king more dead than alive.

Sorrow-stricken, he asked Sumantra "Where is my dear son? Where have you left him? I can't live without him!" With these words, he lost consciousness.

As grief-laden days passed by slowly, Dasharatha remembered something that had happened long ago and thinking of which increased his anguish. He unburdened his heart to Kaushalya, saying, "No one can escape the fruit of one's action. I now endure the result of a great sin that I had committed in my youth. Now the time has come for me to repay."

With this, King Dasharatha narrated an incident from his past, "One evening, I went out to hunt on the banks of River Sarayu. I had the skill to shoot unseen targets, aiming by sound only. I wanted to test myself. As it was a dense forest, I waited for any wild animal to come to the river to drink water. Soon enough, I heard a gurgling sound, as of an elephant drinking water. At once, I aimed an arrow in the direction from where the sound came."

"But I was shocked to hear a human voice exclaim, 'Alas! I am shot!' I rushed to the river, where I was horrified to see that the arrow had not hit an animal, but a young boy who lay in a pool of blood."

Curious, Kaushalya asked him, "Who was this young lad?"

"The young boy was Sharavan Kumar. He was taking his blind parents on a pilgrimage, carrying them on his shoulders in two baskets strung on either end of a long pole. The moment I went near him, he cried, 'O King, why did you aim your arrow at me? I was just taking some water from the river for my parents. My old, blind parents are waiting for me in the grove to quench their thirst; please take this water pitcher to them.' With these words, he breathed his last.

Dasharatha's Last Moments

King Dasharatha continued to narrate the incident, "The next moment, I picked up the pot of water and went to the grove. There, I saw a blind couple eagerly waiting for their son. On hearing my footsteps, the old man said, "Have you brought water, son? Please give it to us, we are very thirsty."

Fearing that I might be recognised, I didn't utter a word, but the old man had sensed that something was wrong. He refused to drink water until I spoke to him. I was left with no other alternative but to reveal my identity and tell them the whole story. Grief-stricken, the old blind parents cried inconsolably. Then the old man said, 'O King, your sin is great indeed. This immense grief you have brought upon us, you too, will endure one day. You will suffer the parting from your son, and that will be the cause of your death.' Saying this, the old man and his wife died in front of me."

By this moment, King Dasharatha was hardly aware of his surroundings. Steeped in sadness, he continued to speak, "My sin has pursued me and I am now in its grip. It is the curse of Shravan Kumar's old blind parents, which has come true today. The messengers of Yama are calling me. My last moment has arrived. O Rama, where are you? Please come and save me! Oh my dear Rama!" Thus uttering Rama's name, the king breathed his last.

Bharata Returns

After King Dasharatha's death, Sage Vashishtha sent messengers to the kingdom of Kekaya, and give Bharata the message that family preceptor and ministers require his presence in Ayodhya. The messengers were instructed not to show any sign of sorrow, and not to disclose about the king's death.

On receiving the message, Bharata accompanied by Shatrughna took leave of his uncle and grandfather and started the journey towards Ayodhya. As the chariot approached the city, Bharata's mind was filled with misgivings. Inauspicious omens were seen everywhere. Bharata concluded that some great misfortune had befallen the city, which must be the reason he had been hastily sent for. The moment they reached the palace, Bharata rushed to Dasharatha's chamber. Not finding him there only increased his anxiety.

He then went to Kaikeyi's chamber. Without wasting a moment, he asked, "Where is the king. The envoys rushed me, saying there was urgent work demanding my presence here. What is it all about?"

Kaikeyi said, "My child, your father had his full share of blessings in this life. His fame was great. He has now entered the higher world and joined the gods."

Hearing these words, Bharata fell down on the ground and started crying like a child in uncontrolled grief.

Looking at her son, Kaikeyi said, "Arise, O King. It is not worthy of a king to mourn like this. Honour and glory are awaiting your acceptance."

══ Intrigue Wasted ══

Innocent at heart, Bharata did not notice what Kaikeyi had said in her appeal.

Grief-stricken Bharata thus asked Kaikeyi, "Before leaving for my uncle's house, I had expected that on return to Ayodhya, I will witness great festive ceremonies in the city with Rama being crowned as Yuvraja. How differently have things turned out! But mother, where is Rama?"

Kaikeyi's answer had to be consistent with truth and her plans. She said, "Dear son, Rama's coronation was announced and everyone was jubilant! However, bound by your love, I asked the king to fulfil the two boons he had granted to me long time back. In my first boon, I asked that you, instead of Rama, should be made the Yuvraja. As my second boon, I asked the king to exile Rama to the forest for a period of fourteen years. Bound by his past promise, the king agreed. Rama has therefore, left for the forest with Sita and Lakshmana."

Bharata was shocked on hearing this tale of jealousy, greed and grief. He cried in anger, "O mother, how can you be so heartless? What sorrow you have brought upon Ayodhya!"

To this Kaikeyi replied, "Do not waste your time in lamentations now. You have inherited your father's kingdom. Attend to what has fallen on you as your duty."

Bharata declared, "I am not going to be a part of your devious plan. I'll never accept this crown as it belongs to my brother Rama. If it had not been your greed, today my father would have been alive and Rama would have been the Yuvraja. But I will amend your wrongs. I am going to the forest to bring back Rama!"

With this, he ordered Sumantra to get the army ready, "We will proceed to the forest to bring Rama back home!"

The next morning, leading a large army, Bharata started the journey towards Sage Bharadwaja's ashrama. When he reached the banks of River Ganga, Guha, the hunter-king, came to pay him a customary visit.

To him Bharata said, "I wish to proceed to the hermitage of Bharadwaja. We do not know the way, and we also need help to cross this great river."

Guha bowed and assured him of providing assistance in addressing both the challenges. However, he was suspicious of Bharata's intentions. Politely, he asked, "You must excuse me for expressing a doubt which occurs to me on seeing the large army accompanying you. Surely you have no hostile intentions towards Rama?"

Pained by these words, Bharata said, "Have no misgivings, Guha. Rama is my father now, for he has taken the place of my lost father. I have come here to request him to return back to Ayodhya."

Guha rejoiced to see such intense love for Rama in Bharata's eyes.

With the assistance of Guha's men, Bharata and his army crossed River Ganga. From a distance, they saw a beautiful grove with a cottage in its midst. Bharata accompanied by sage Vashishtha went to the ashrama and offered humble salutations to Sage Bharadwaja.

Looking at Bharata, the sage said, "Bharata, your grief is not hidden from me! May you be successful in your noble intentions. Rama, along with Sita and Lakshmana, is dwelling on Chitrakuta hill. Rest here for the night and tomorrow you can resume your journey."

The Brothers Meet

The next morning, Bharata took leave of the sage and proceeded towards the Chitrakuta hill. On the slope of the hill, they spotted a beautiful hut, indicating the spot where Rama and Sita along with Lakshmana were residing. When Bharata and his convoy reached the cottage, they found Rama, Lakshmana and Sita sitting outside the hut.

Without wasting a moment, Bharata rushed to meet Rama. He fell at

Rama's feet and said, "Please forgive me! It is because the wrongs of my mother that you are forced to stay in this forest."

"Rama embraced Bharata and said, "O beloved brother, why did you leave Ayodhya and our father's side? Why have you come all this way to the forest?"

To this Bharata replied, "Dear brother, why do you ask me about the kingdom? The kingdom belongs to you. You are the rightful king! Come with me to Ayodhya, wear the crown and shower your grace on our family and people."

After a brief pause, Bharata broke the dreadful news, "I can no more stay at the side of our father! When you left Ayodhya for the forest and before I returned from Kekaya, the king embraced death, slain by the grief of separation from you."

Hearing this, Lakshmana started crying like a child! On the other hand, Rama stood calm, his face conveying no emotion.

Once again, Bharata pleaded, "Only you can save us. Undo all the evil that has been done and wipe off our tears by agreeing to be crowned.

Without a rightful king, the land is desolate and helpless. I fall at your feet and beg you. Do not refuse, O brother!"

Saying this, with tear-filled eyes, Bharata clung to Rama's feet.

Rama raised his brother from the ground, and embracing him, said, "Our duty is to honour our father and mother. It is your duty to rule the land. And I too shall do my duty and fulfil our father's last command by living fourteen years in the Dandaka forest. I will return to Ayodhya only after that."

Thus, Rama remained obstinate. But Bharata was equally adamant.

He said, "I will stay in the forest instead. You must return to Ayodhya."

Together the three brothers, Lakshmana, Bharata and Shatrughna offered to stay in the forest to fulfill their father's wish and make Rama return to Ayodhya. However, this too couldn't shake Rama's resolve. His father's word was of great importance, therefore, he remained firm.

Finally, Bharata had to give up and accept that Rama would not return to Ayodhya before fourteen years. He said, "Next to our father, you are my father. Your wish is my command."

"As per your wish, I will rule," he declared, "but only in your name. I will not sit on the throne. I shall stay outside the city and discharge the king's duties in your place. Till you return, I shall take your sandals with me and place them on the throne. They will symbolise your presence and rule over Ayodhya till the day you return."

"So be it," answered Rama. With this, Bharata took leave of Rama. Carrying the sandals on his head, he started his journey towards Ayodhya.

Off to Panchavati

When Bharata left for Ayodhya, Rama too decided to leave Chitrakuta hill and move deeper into the forest. Though it was a beautiful place, still the memories of Bharata and the news of Dasharatha's death made him restless. So Rama, Sita and Lakshmana started their journey towards Sage Atri's hermitage, where they received a pleasant welcome by the sage himself and his wife Anusuya.

After resting for the night at the ashrama Rama, Sita and Lakshmana resumed their journey in the morning. Soon they reached the hermitage of Sage Sutikshna. Sage Sutikshna was a disciple of Sage Agastya.

The two princes and Sita were welcomed by the sage with open arms. Later in the day, when they were resting after a meal, Sage Sutikshna told Rama about the atrocities of demons in Dandaka forest. He also told them to meet his guru, Sage Agastya, whose hermitage was not far away, as he could suggest a suitable place for them to settle down. Taking leave of Sage Sutikshna, they started their journey towards Sage Agastya's hermitage. They received a heart-warming welcome by Sage Agastya. Rama expressed his gratitude for the hospitality received and asked him to suggest a place where they could settle down and live in peace. After a moment's thought, Sage Agastya said, "There is one such place not far from here. It is called Panchavati. Close to River Godavari, surrounded by abundant greenery, it is home to different kinds of animals. You will find it a pleasant place to stay."

Before leaving for Panchavati, Sage Agastya gave Rama the bow made by Vishwakarma for Vishnu, an inexhaustible quiver, and a sword to slay the demons. With the sage's blessings, Rama, Sita and Lakshmana set off on their journey towards Panchavati.

On their way to Panchavati, they met a huge vulture like bird perched on a big tree.

"Who are you?" asked Rama.

The vulture answered affectionately, "My child, I am Jatayu, your father's old friend."

He further added, "When you leave Sita alone and go for hunting in the forest, I shall take care of her safety."

Pleased to hear this, the prince accepted the offer of the bird with gratitude. They then continued their journey.

As they walked on, the path began to climb up. And soon, they reached a scenic hilly area. This was Panchavati. Rama was charmed by the beauty of the place, which had greenery all around, trees laden with flowers, birds singing melodiously and a river glistening around the hills.

Looking at Lakshmana, Rama said, "We can build our cottage here and enjoy our stay here for any length of time."

Lakshmana soon built a beautiful hut and they settled down in Panchavati. Life in Panchavati was peaceful and blissful. Early morning, they would go to River Godavari to bathe and offer morning prayers to Sun God. Then they would gather fruits from the trees, drink water from the spring, and enjoy their meal. On some days, they would just sit, whiling away time, talking about old days and tales of long ago.

Soorpanakha's Proposal

Time passed and soon ten years rolled by. Sita was happily settled in Panchavati, and hardly missed her palace life. However, this peaceful life was not to last long.

Soorpanakha, the evil sister of demon king Ravana, roamed in the forest, hunting for wild animals. One day, she came across Rama's abode.

Looking at the royal prince sitting outside the hut, she fell in love with him. "What a handsome man! I must marry him!" she said to herself. The next moment, she changed herself into a beautiful woman and approached Rama.

"O handsome man! I am Soorpanakha, the sister of demon king Ravana. The lords of this region, Khara and Dushana, are also my brothers. The moment I set my eyes on you, I fell in love with you! I am the woman you deserve. Come with me as my husband."

Amused to hear this, Rama smiled and said, "Lady, I cannot marry you as I'm already married. Here is my wife." With these words, he pointed towards Sita who was sitting nearby. "But, I have a younger brother, who is more handsome than me."

Soorpanakha turned to approach Lakshmana, who was watching with a mischievous smile.

"Alright, I'll marry him," said Soorpanakha as she held Lakshmana's arm.

Lakshmana entered into the humour of the situation and said, "Do not be foolish. I am just a slave to my brother, while you are a princess.

How could you become my wife and accept the position of a slave yourself? Insist on Rama to take you as his second wife!"

As told by Lakshmana, Soorpanakha went again to Rama, who again declined her offer.

Enraged, pointing to Sita, she said, "It is this wretched woman who stands between you and me. I will kill her this very moment!" With these words, she leapt towards Sita. The next minute, she attained her demon form.

Rama called out to Lakshmana, "You teach her a lesson, I am taking Sita inside the hut."

Lakshmana pulled out his sword, and with lightning speed, cut off Soorpanakha's nose and the tips of her long ears. Soorpanakha screamed in pain, uttered a loud wail, and disappeared into the forest.

Khara and Dushana are Killed

Soorpanakha went straight to her brothers Khara and Dushana and told him, "I was wandering in the forest when I saw two young princes accompanied by a woman. I went to ask them, by what intent they roamed around in the forest where no one dares to enter? But as soon as they saw me, they chopped off my nose and ears. Oh brother, avenge my insult!"

Hearing this story, Khara and Dushana ordered their generals, "Go at once! Slay these men and bring their lifeless bodies!"

Thus accompanied by some of the ferocious

warriors, Soorpanakha returned to Panchavati, determined to avenge her insult. It did not take long for Rama's arrows to annihilate the demon generals. Once again, lamenting loudly, Soorpanakha went to her brothers. This time Khara and Dushana themselves decided to lead their armies and started towards Panchavati. A ferocious battle then ensued between the demon army and the sons of Dasharatha. Soon, the whole army was destroyed and only Khara remained. Seeing the poor condition of Khara, Dushana came forward to help him, but Rama cut his both hands and killed all his army. Seeing his brother thrashing about, Khara directed his chariot against Rama. The arrows shot by the two warriors covered the sky.

Rama took up the bow of Vishnu, aimed at Khara, and cut his bow in two. Khara then took his mace and and tried to throw it at Rama. The mace was split by Rama's arrows into splinters. Without further delay, Rama aimed deadly arrows at Khara, which finally killed him.

The Path of Ruin

Soorpanakha then fled to Lanka, to seek aid from her brother, demon king Ravana.

Ravana sat on his throne surrounded by his ministers. Suddenly, there appeared before him, his sister Soorpanakha, mutilated and bleeding, crying in pain, sorrow and shame. Everyone present in the court was horror-struck. Once again she narrated the whole story.

"Rama, son of Dasharatha, single handedly, slaughtered the entire demon army, and killed my brother Khara. O demon king, Ravana, would you not avenge the death of your brother and humiliation faced by your sister? Have you no thoughts of vengeance, you, a hero, a brother, a king?"

Stung by her words and his heart struck by his sister's suffering and sorrow, Ravana said, "Be sure you shall have revenge! To avenge my sister, who has suffered so much pain and shame, I will carry off Rama's wife. I will strike his honour as he did mine by hurting my sister." With this resolve, Ravana went to meet Mareecha, and said, "To avenge my sister, I have decided to carry off Rama's wife from Dandaka forest, and for this I seek your help. You should change your form into a golden deer and roam around Rama's cottage attracting Sita's attention. She will surely insist on Rama and Lakshmana pursuing and catching you for her. When they are thus engaged and she is left alone, I will execute my plan."

The Golden Deer

It was a bright morning. Sita was busy gathering flowers from the garden outside their hut, when her attention was caught by the golden deer. Stuck by the beauty of the magical creature, Sita said to Rama, "Please catch this deer for me! We shall bring it up as a pet. This is the most beautiful creature I have seen so far in this forest!"

Rama took his bow and arrows and decided to pursue the deer. Before leaving, he told Lakshmana, "Brother, don't leave Sita's side and guard her vigilantly. I will be back soon." With this, Rama went in pursuit of the golden deer. In order to give Ravana plenty of time to execute his devious plan, Mareecha led Rama deep into the forest far away from his hut. Rama, tired of the pursuit, bent his bow and sent forth an arrow, which pierced the deer. Mareecha resumed his natural form and simulating Rama's voice, called out, "Ah Sita, Ah Lakshmana!" and fell dead.

Lakshmana and Sita both heard Rama's voice.

Trembling with fear, Sita said to Lakshmana, "There, Lakshmana, do you not hear your brother's voice? Go, go at once! Do not delay!" Lakshmana was aware about the deceitful nature of demons. Obeying his brother's command, he resolved not to go to the forest.

At this Sita grew furious. "Son of Sumitra! Have you too turned to foe? Have you been with us waiting only for your brother to die? Why else do you stand here and refuse to go to his rescue when he cries for help. Oh, how completely have you been deceiving us, Rama and me, all these years!"

These cruel words pierced Lakshmana's heart like poisoned arrows.

Lakshmana tried to pacify Sita, saying, "It is some trick. Do not be deceived and grieve for nothing. Rama has asked me not to leave your side. Don't ask me to leave you alone and go. I cannot disobey my brother."

Wounded by Sita's words, Lakshmana was forced to yield. He said, "I'm going into the forest, but listen to me carefully. Before leaving, I will draw a holy line, Lakshmana Rekha. Please do not cross the line until either of us returns. As long as you don't cross the line, you will be safe. If anyone else tries to cross this line, he will burn down to ashes."

With these words, Lakshmana left to look for Rama.

Sita's Abduction

When Lakshmana left, Ravana who was waiting for this opportunity, disguised as a hermit, arrived at Sita's doorstep.

He called out, "Alms for the hermit! O kind lady, please give some alms to this hermit."

Hearing the plea of the hermit, Sita went inside the cottage and brought some fruits on a leaf. She placed the leaf on the ground outside the Lakshmana Rekha and didn't step outside. Ravana refused to touch the offerings thus given.

"I'm not a beggar. Come out here and give the alms respectfully in my hands."

Sita hesitated and said, "I can't cross the Lakshmana Rekha. Please accept the alms."

Hearing this, Ravana said, "I will not accept it until you give me with your own hands."

Sita yielded and stepped out of the Lakshmana Rekha to give the fruits to the old hermit. The next moment, clouds roared, lightning flashed, and the Lakshmana Rekha itself burst into flames.

Ravana stepped forward and grabbed Sita's hand. As he touched her, he resumed his natural form, ten heads appeared and danced like hooded cobras. Sita tried to pull back but Ravana's grip was firm. He gave a thundering cry of rage and in a flash he pulled her into his Pushpaka Vimana, the flying golden chariot.

The next moment, they were high up in the sky. "Rama, O Rama, help me! Lakshmana, help me!" cried Sita. Her cries were heard by none other than Jatayu, who was half asleep on a tree. Recognising it to be Sita's voice, Jatayu rushed to her aid.

Brave Jatayu

Jatayu called out to Ravana, "O demon king, I am Jatayu, the king of eagles. Give up this wicked act! If you don't leave Sita, I will not allow you to fly past me. Step down from your chariot and fight, if you are not a coward!"

Hearing this, Ravana flared up in rage. He aimed his deadly arrows at Jatayu, but the clever eagle intercepted them all and with his talons tore Ravana's flesh. However, in front of Ravana's arrows, Jatayu could not sustain for long. He attacked the chariot and smashed its wheel. With this, the chariot fell on to the ground.

The gallant bird tried hard to wrench off Ravana's arm which held Sita. However, Ravana had twenty arms. Every time an arm was pulled off, it was replaced by a new one.

At last, Ravana took out his sword and aimed a mighty blow on Jatayu's wings and talons. The old bird now lay helpless on the ground. The next moment, Ravana's chariot again rose in the air, with Sita struggling in his hold.

In Search of Sita

Meanwhile, in the other part of the forest, Mareecha the demon was struck by Rama's arrow. He had transformed into his original form of a demon before dying. At once, Rama realised that the demon had fooled them. 'Alas, we have been deceived! It would be terrible if Lakshmana is also deceived by his cry and leaves Sita alone for my rescue!'

With this thought, Rama rushed back to the hut. On the way, he saw Lakshmana running towards him. Panicked, and anticipating the approaching danger, Rama asked, "Why did you leave Sita alone in the forest, Lakshmana?"

Lakshmana narrated how Sita forced him to leave the hut for Rama's rescue. Rama told him how the golden deer turned out to be a demon.

Worried about the danger around the corner, Rama and Lakshmana rushed towards the hut. The hut was strangely quiet and Sita was nowhere to be seen. They were distraught at not finding Sita anywhere and decided to move out into the forest to continue their search.

The two princes searched every mountain, forest and riverbank calling Sita's name aloud. But all in vain. They did not so much as find a clue anywhere. A herd of deer, however, moving southwards seemed to indicate to Rama and Lakshmana that they too should travel in the same direction. They did so, and after a while, found gold beads from Sita's jewels scattered on the way. Soon they came upon a broken wheel of a chariot.

The two princes looked at the wheel when Rama spotted a bunch of torn feathers dripping with blood, near a tree. At that very moment, they heard a sharp cry of pain! It was Jatayu, severely wounded, counting his last breaths. In a feeble voice, Jatayu said, "The dear princess you are searching for has been carried off by Ravana. Seeing Sita in his Pushpaka Vimana, I intercepted it and gave him a strong fight. However, my age against his youth, my beak and talons against his mighty arrows and heavenly weapons, were no match. As a last blow, he cut off my wings and legs. He then flew off with Sita in the southern direction."

With these words, Jatayu breathed his last.

After performing Jatayu's last rites, Rama and Lakshmana started their journey towards the south. Passing through the forest, they encountered Kabandha, a celestial headless creature. Kabandha was stuck in the body of a demon due to a curse given to him by Sage Sthulashiras.

When Rama struck him with a golden arrow, Kabandha attained salvation. Before departing to heaven, he said to Rama, "Go to the beautiful banks of River Pampa and seek the help of monkey king Sugriva. Driven out of the kingdom by his brother Vali, he lives in Rishyamukha hill. Gain his friendship, and he will help you in finding Sita." Saying this, Kabandha disappeared. And now, Rama and Lakshmana started their journey towards Pampa in search of Sugriva. As the sun set and darkness descended, the two princes spotted a hermitage at a distance and decided to break their journey to take some rest.

Shabari's Berries

It was getting dark. Rama and Lakshmana were tired from the long journey. They decided to take some rest at the hermitage on the way. It belonged to Shabari, a disciple of Sage Matanga.

Shabari was overwhelmed with joy to see the two princes, and received them with great devotion. She washed their tired feet and said, "My dear lords, you must be very hungry!"

Then she went inside to look for food suitable for the princes. However, all she could find were some berries. She brought them out for Rama and Lakshmana to eat.

But, before giving the berries to the two brothers, Shabari would taste them. If the berry was sweet, she would give it to Rama, who ate the same with a smile on his face. If the berry was bitter, Shabari threw it away. In this manner, she went on tasting every berry before handing it over.

While Rama ate the berries happily, Lakshmana was finding it difficult to eat the half eaten berries by Shabari.

When Shabari went inside to bring some more berries, Lakshmana asked Rama, "How could you eat her half-eaten berries?"

Hearing this, Rama smiled and said, "Dear brother, you only saw the half-eaten berries but forgot to notice her devotion. She wants to offer me only the sweet berries. Therefore, she tastes the berries, offering me the sweet ones and throwing away the bitter ones. She is my true devotee."

This made Lakshmana see the truth. After that, he didn't hesitate to eat half-eaten berries offered by old Shabari.

After resting for a while, Rama and Lakshmana again began their journey, in search of Sugriva, the monkey king.

Rama Sugriva Alliance

Rama and Lakshmana finally reached Rishyamukha hill. Sugriva, who was hiding in fear of his elder brother Vali, saw the two well-armed strangers roaming around in the forest.

He said to Hanuman, his minister, "Hanuman, I see someone coming towards us. I wonder who has sent them!"

Sugriva feared that Vali was following him in disguise, in order to kill him. Or else, he had sent his warriors to kill him. So he sent Hanuman to find out more about the two strangers.

Disguised as a brahmin, Hanuman went to Rama, in order to know more about them and understand the purpose of their visit. Rama looked up and smiled at Hanuman. Rama's smile evoked a strange sensation in Hanuman's heart, which made him change into his original form.

Hanuman said, "My Lord, I do not know who you are but your presence makes my heart fill with unknown joy. I am Hanuman, minister of Sugriva. I came here on order of my chief, who wants to know who you are and what is the purpose of your visit."

To this Rama said, "It is indeed fortunate that you came here. He whom we are searching for is himself looking for us! We came here to seek Sugriva's help. My wife, Sita, has been abducted by Ravana. We want Sugriva's help to rescue her. We seek the friendship of your king. Hanuman, can you take us to Sugriva?"

Hanuman happily offered, "Please sit on my shoulders. I will carry you both to my chief."

With these words, Hanuman carried them to where Sugriva waited for him.

Hanuman introduced the two princes to Sugriva. After exchanging customary greetings, Hanuman said to Sugriva, "Rama, the son of King Dasharatha seeks your help. He has come here to make an alliance with you to find his wife Sita."

Stretching forth his hand to Rama, Sugriva said, "O Prince, if you care for the friendship of a vanara, here is my hand, accept it."

Rama clasped his hand and embraced him. Hanuman, meanwhile, gathered some wood and kindled a fire. After worshipping it with flowers, he placed the blazing fire between Rama and Sugriva as a symbol of their alliance. The two of them walked around the fire to turn their new friendship into a long-lasting alliance.

Then Sugriva narrated the story of his life to Rama. Sugriva and his elder brother Vali were once devoted to each other. However, fate had something else in store. Once a demon named Mayavi came to Kishkindha, the capital city, and challenged Vali to an instant combat.

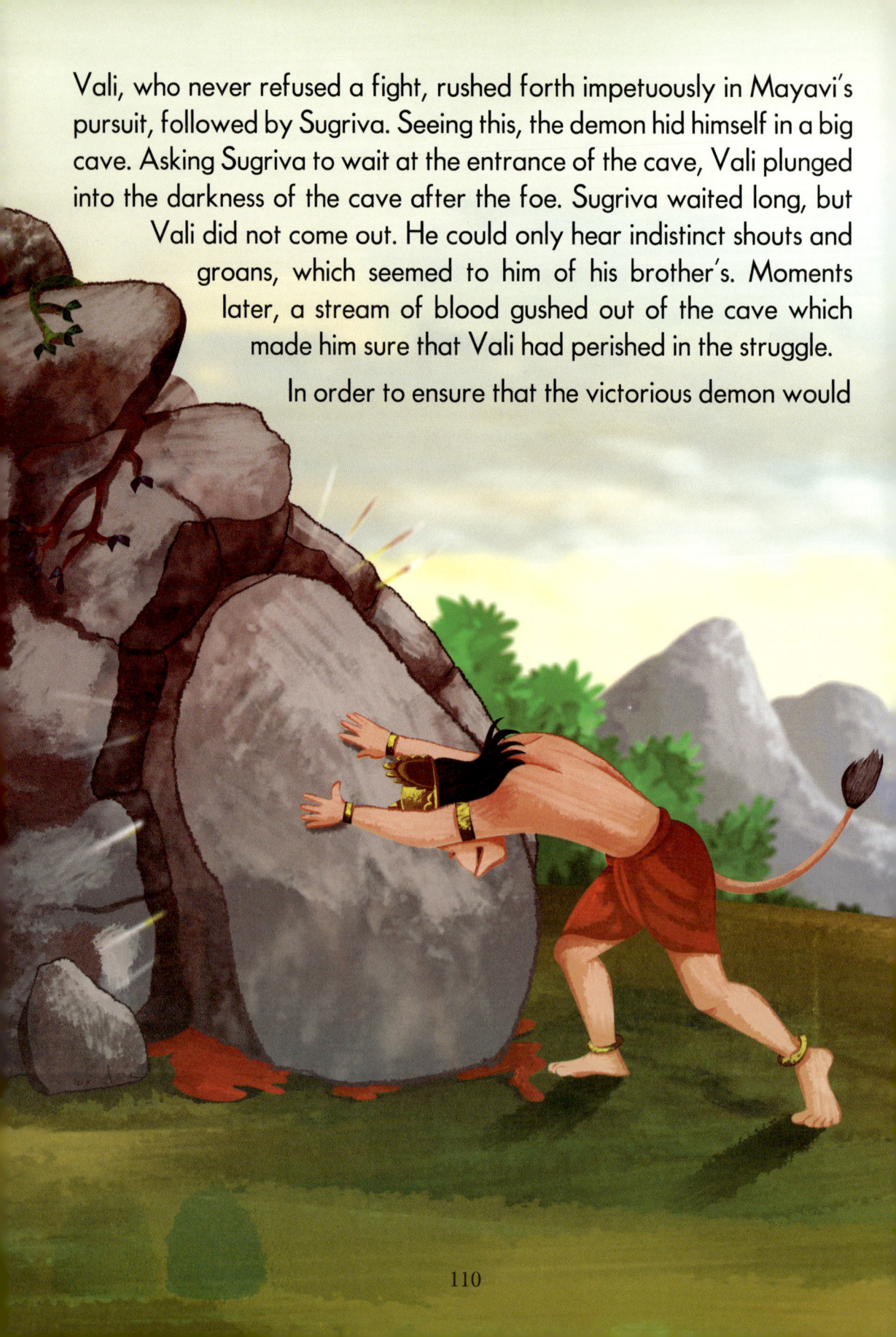

Vali, who never refused a fight, rushed forth impetuously in Mayavi's pursuit, followed by Sugriva. Seeing this, the demon hid himself in a big cave. Asking Sugriva to wait at the entrance of the cave, Vali plunged into the darkness of the cave after the foe. Sugriva waited long, but Vali did not come out. He could only hear indistinct shouts and groans, which seemed to him of his brother's. Moments later, a stream of blood gushed out of the cave which made him sure that Vali had perished in the struggle.

In order to ensure that the victorious demon would

not rush out in elation and destroy Kishkindha, Sugriva blocked the entrance of the cave with a huge rock and returned home with the story of Vali's death. Thus, he became the king of Kishkindha.

While he was enjoying the fruits of kingship, Vali returned, filled with wrath. Accusing Sugriva of betrayal and treason, Vali drove him out of the kingdom.

Hearing his story, Rama said, "I shall help you regain your lost glory. That's my promise to you. We shall plan out a strategy for finding Sita, but first, we must deal with your brother, Vali."

The Slaying of Vali

It was decided that next day Sugriva will challenge Vali for a single combat. As planned, Sugriva went to the palace alone to challenge Vali. Rama and Lakshmana stayed back, hiding behind the trees.

Outside the palace gates, Sugriva let out a mighty roar and challenged Vali, "Vali, this is your brother Sugriva. I have come here to seek revenge for your cruelties towards me. You took away my home, my wife and my people from me. Come out and fight!"

Vali, who was then resting, was startled with Sugriva's unexpected behaviour. Overwhelmed with rage, he went outside the palace gates to face Sugriva.

"If you love your life," warned Vali, "run away!"

Sugriva retorted angrily and the battle began. Angry with the ill treatment meted out by his brother and remembering the past wrongs, Sugriva maintained an equal combat for long. However, Vali's greater might soon began to prevail and it seemed that Sugriva was in great distress. Assessing the situation, Rama stood behind the tree prepared with his bow, as he knew Sugriva couldn't hold much longer.

Just as Vali was about to strangle Sugriva, Rama shot a deadly arrow at Vali's mighty chest. Vali crashed down.

Lying down on the ground, Vali looked at Rama and asked, "You are a son of King Dasharatha. The world is full of praises for your valour and virtue. And yet, while I was engaged in a battle with Sugriva, you came unseen, from behind, and shot a fatal arrow at me. For a royal prince to kill an innocent person in this way, isn't it a grievous sin? Isn't it against dharma?"

To this Rama replied gently, "My dear Vali, you have not understood the meaning of dharma. If you had, you wouldn't have transgressed the boundaries defined by it. You have been unjust towards your brother and defied dharma by taking away his wife."

Further Rama added, "Sugriva is my friend, whom I promised to help. I can't go back on my promise."

Rama's words opened Vali's eyes. With folded hands, he said to Rama, "I deserve the punishment of ill-treating my younger brother. But before I leave, I would like to request you to treat my son Angada and Sugriva alike. I also request you to ensure that Sugriva is not harsh towards my wife Tara, as she is not to be blamed for the sins I committed." With these words, the mighty king Vali breathed his last. Soon Sugriva was crowned as the king of Kishkindha. As promised to Vali, he made his son Angada the Yuvraja. Peace, happiness and harmony were once again restored at Kishkindha.

The Search Begins

The rainy season had started. The search for Sita had to be suspended for some time, as the forest paths were flooded.

Once the rain stopped, Hanuman approached Sugriva and said, "You have regained the kingdom of your ancestors and are in secure possession of it. However, something still needs to be done. You must fulfil your promise to your allies. The rainy season is over. We should not delay the task of searching Sita any further. Didn't Rama kill your enemy promptly? We should also fulfil our promise with equal promptness."

The next day, in the presence of Rama and Lakshmana, Sugriva called all his army generals including Nala, Angada, Hanuman, and Jambavan to brief them about their course of action in the search. However, he had a strong belief that only Hanuman could execute this task. Therefore, he took him aside and said, "Son of Vayu, possessing the strength and splendour of your father, you alone can succeed in this task. I rely on you to take up the duty of finding Sita."

Next, Sugriva issued orders to his army, "Sita must be found anyhow. No matter where she is hidden, you must find her. Return within a month with news of her!"

With this order, the army swarmed out like ants from an anthill and spread in four directions. Satabali and his army proceeded northwards; Vinata went east; Sushena westwards; Hanuman, Angada and Tara started their journey towards south.

Before Hanuman started on his journey, Rama gave his ring to him and said, "Take this ring. I have full faith that you will find Sita. This ring will tell her that you are my messenger."

Soon, a month passed by. The army that went in north, east and west directions, returned in a month and reported that Sita was not be found anywhere. However, Hanuman who had gone southward, in the direction where Ravana had taken Sita, had not returned. Therefore, Rama was still hopeful!

In search of Sita, Hanuman had reached the seashore with his army. Angada, who had lost all hopes of finding Sita, said to Hanuman, "Because of Dasharatha, Rama had to dwell in the forest. Ravana carried off Sita. The heroic Jatayu lost his life in the attempt to save Sita. By fate did all these things happen and the end of the tale is that we are dying here. We will never be able to find Sita, and returning empty handed will bring us disgrace. In what curious ways does fate work!"

Sampati Helps

On a hill nearby, sat Sampati, the vulture king who had lost his wings and was unable to move. Sampati overheard Angada thus lamenting.

At the mention of Jatayu, he wished to hear the complete story. "Who brings the sad news of my dear brother Jatayu?" he cried in agony.

"O vanaras, is beloved Jatayu dead indeed? Was Jatayu killed by Ravana? Tell me all!"

Hearing Sampati's plea, Angada narrated the complete story and asked the old bird if he could help Rama in any way. Sampati, though old and weak, had very powerful eyes. He said to Hanuman, "Sitting here on this rock, I can see very far. Wait here, I will hop on to a higher rock and look into the city of Lanka to find Sita." Hearing this, the whole army was excited. Few moments later, Sampati announced, "I can see Sita sitting in the Ashoka Vatika in the city of Lanka. If you can manage to cross this sea, you will definitely find her."

Sampati's troubles were now over. He had received a boon that when he would help Rama, he would get back his wings. The boon came true as the young feathers began to grow. Sampati now shone with fresh beauty. Taking leave of the vanaras, Sampati flew away.

122

The Son of Vayu

"How can we cross the sea, enter Lanka, see Sita and return?" Hanuman and his army wondered.

It was at this moment that Angada suggested, "I feel that the son of Vayu, Hanuman, is the best in strength and skill to perform this deed."

He further addressed Hanuman and said, "O Hanuman! Realise your true strength and spring forward! You can cross the sea in a single jump. Accomplish the task and end our troubles."

Old Jambavan also praised Hanuman and reminded him of his childhood heroic deed when he had swallowed the Sun. Reminded of his strength, at once Hanuman's form began to swell like the sea in high tide. As the vanaras watched, Hanuman kept on increasing in size.

On attaining his full strength, Hanuman offered prayers to Surya, Indra, Vayu, Brahma, and then closed his eyes and thought of Lord Rama. Then with a roar of triumph, he rose into the sky. The entire vanara army watched the grandeur of Hanuman's magnificent deed, spellbound.

A Fascinating Leap

Hanuman flew at great speed with his arms outstretched. Beneath him his shadow seemed like a ship sailing in the sea. The Ocean God was aware about the purpose for which Hanuman was undertaking the long journey to Lanka. He wanted to extend assistance to Hanuman who was serving Lord Rama in finding Sita.

Thus, the Ocean God bade Mainaka, the hidden mountain under the surface of the sea, "Mainaka, rise above the surface of the sea, so that

Hanuman can rest on you for a while before resuming his long journey towards Lanka."

Mainaka rose from the ocean. Thinking that Hanuman will come to rest, Mainaka Mountain covered itself with trees laden with fruits. However, when Hanuman saw the mountain, he perceived it as an obstacle in his path. He thrust his chest forward and knocked the mountain over.

Mainaka Mountain took the form of a human and said, "I'm sorry, if I appear as an obstacle in your path. Following the orders of the Ocean God, I rose to help you. O son of Vayu, take some rest on the mountain and then continue your journey."

"I'm sorry to have hurt you. I cannot stop! My vow to fulfil Rama's purpose permits no delay," said Hanuman as he rushed past Mainaka.

However, little did Hanuman know that another obstacle awaited him in the form of Sursa.

Sursa, the mother of serpents, took the form of an ugly demon, and rose from the ocean's depths. She stopped Hanuman and said, "I have been blessed with a boon that no one can get past me without entering my mouth."

To this Hanuman said, "I am on a crucial journey. Do not stop me!"

"Impossible!" said the monster. "You must enter my mouth."

Seeing no option, Hanuman expanded his form and grew bigger and bigger. Sursa too opened her mouth wider and wider. When her mouth was thus wide open, the next moment, Hanuman contracted his body to the size of a thumb, and flew into the demon's mouth. With equal swiftness, he came out again and resumed his former normal form.

He then laughed and said, "You have fulfilled your wish, mother. I have entered your mouth. What more do you need?"

To this Sursa said, "You have my blessings now. Your effort will be crowned with success."

Thus surviving many trials, Hanuman flew across the ocean and reached the coast of Lanka.

Hanuman Reaches Lanka

Filled with hope, Hanuman set foot in Lanka. But soon the moment of triumph and accomplishment of the journey was overshadowed by apprehension.

"I have crossed the sea, but this is only the beginning of my mission. There, on mount Trikuta, stands Ravana's magnificent city. How beautiful, how rich, how well secured it is! How will I find Sita in this huge city without being noticed," thought Hanuman. The next moment, he shrank to the size of a little monkey, no bigger than a cat.

By now the sun had set. The little vanara walked towards the fortress gate. Vowing that the demons should be destroyed, Hanuman entered the fortress of Lanka.

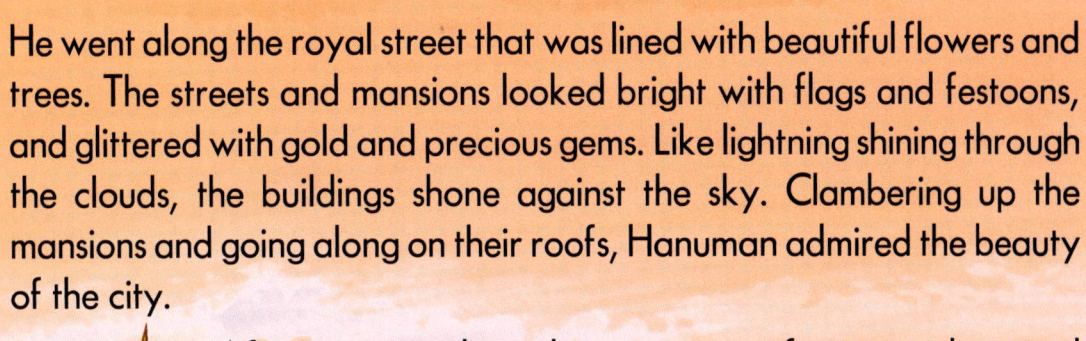

He went along the royal street that was lined with beautiful flowers and trees. The streets and mansions looked bright with flags and festoons, and glittered with gold and precious gems. Like lightning shining through the clouds, the buildings shone against the sky. Clambering up the mansions and going along on their roofs, Hanuman admired the beauty of the city.

After passing through many magnificent gardens and mansions, Hanuman came to a great palace rising in a nobility of splendour far more magnificent than all the other buildings around. It was none other than Ravana's palace.

Hanuman jumped over the walls unnoticed and entered the palace. He looked around, searching for Sita, but she was nowhere to be found. In the inner chambers, Hanuman saw beautiful women adorned in beautiful jewels and fine clothes, sleeping peacefully. Hanuman reasoned that none of these women could be Sita, as after separation from Rama, she would never adorn herself in fineries, nor would sleep in peace.

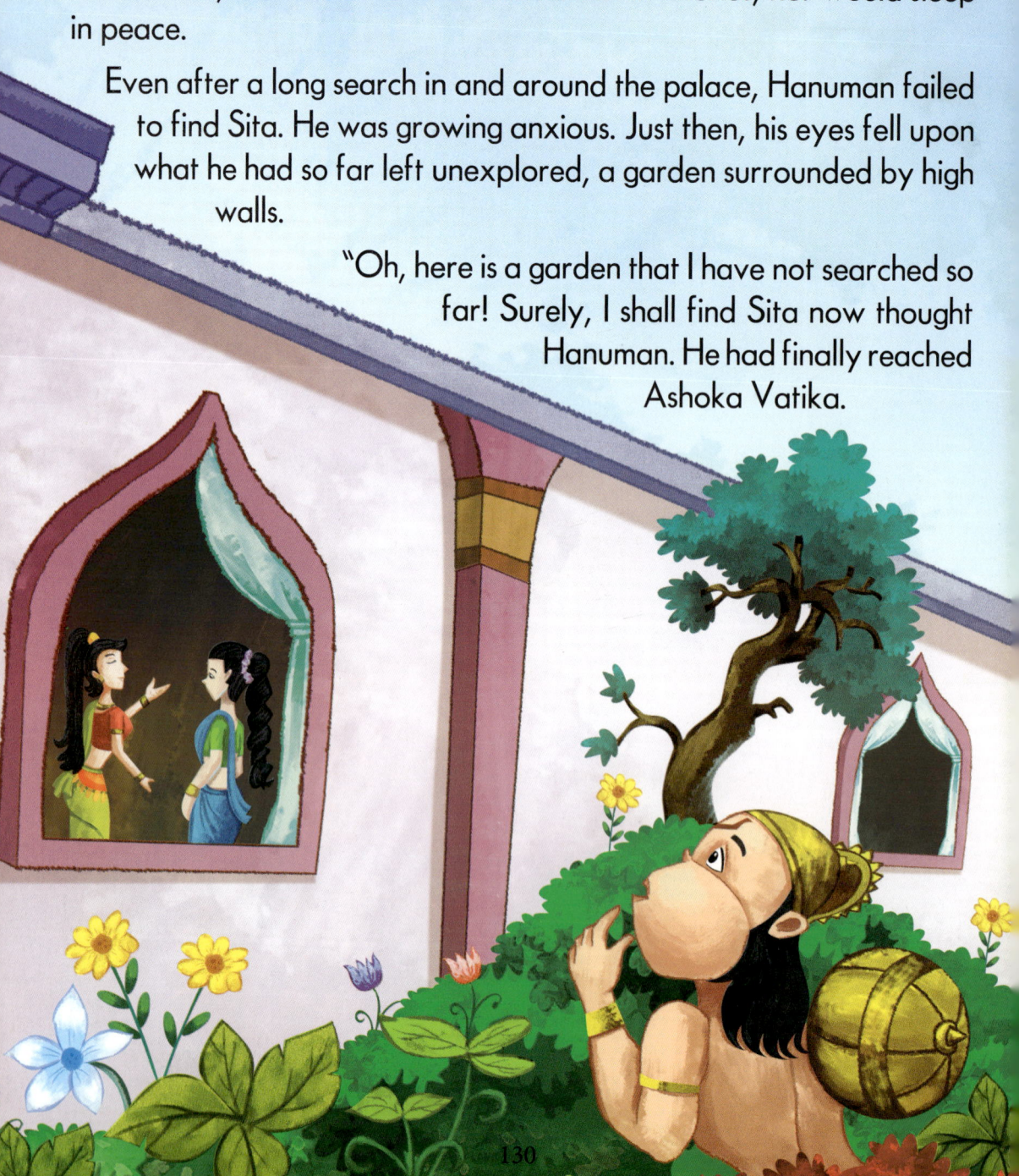

Even after a long search in and around the palace, Hanuman failed to find Sita. He was growing anxious. Just then, his eyes fell upon what he had so far left unexplored, a garden surrounded by high walls.

"Oh, here is a garden that I have not searched so far! Surely, I shall find Sita now thought Hanuman. He had finally reached Ashoka Vatika.

Ashoka Vatika

Ashoka Vatika was an immensely beautiful grove of Ashoka trees. Beautiful flowers, waterfalls, trees laden with delicious fruits, and little bells suspended from the trees filled air with melodious music.

Hanuman climbed up a tree in the garden and sat hidden among its leaves. He looked around. Suddenly, he saw a lady sitting on a pavilion, surrounded by demonesses. Though she looked pale and thin, yet she shone like moon. Her face was bathed in tears, and she seemed to be in deep sorrow.

Looking at her, Hanuman said, "This image of beautiful despair is surely Sita!" The next moment, Hanuman saw the demon king, Ravana, approaching.

Ravana walked towards Sita and said, "O beautiful one! Why do you waste your thoughts on wretched Rama, wandering in the forest? Marry me! My wealth, my kingdom, all shall be yours to enjoy."

To this, Sita replied, "Ravana, do not violate dharma. Do not tread the path of sin. I belong to Rama. Don't invite your ruin! Rama is generous and will surely forgive you if you seek his mercy. Seek forgiveness and safety. Do not seek death and destruction."

Ravana grew angry on hearing these words. He said, "O Sita, you repay my loving words with insults. I will give you two months. Change your mind before they pass. Marry me and be my wife." Saying so, Ravana left.

Sita broke down and sobbed like a child. Hidden amongst the branches of a tree, Hanuman quietly watched the whole scene. As swiftly as he could, Hanuman swung through the branches and hopped on to a branch right above Sita.

He decided to recite in a sweet low tone, the story and virtues of Rama to restore Sita's courage. The next moment, he began chanting Rama's name in a soft voice and started narrating the story of Rama's life.

Hanuman Meets Sita

The sweet words thus uttered by Hanuman filled Sita with delight. She looked around to find who was singing Rama's virtues. Just then, Hanuman descended to the ground and stood before Sita, palms joined and head bent in salutation.

"Who are you? How do you know my lord Rama?" Sita asked Hanuman. To this, Hanuman replied, "I am Hanuman, the servant of Lord Rama. I have been sent to enquire about your welfare by Lord Rama himself."

Sita said, "O vanara! Are you indeed a messenger sent by Rama? How can I believe that you are not Ravana in disguise?"

Hanuman understood her doubts and fears, therefore, he took out the ring given to him by Rama and placed it on Sita's palm. Seeing her husband's ring, Sita's eyes filled with tears.

She cried, "O dear Hanuman, please tell me how is my lord? When is he coming to rescue me from this place?"

Hanuman could not bear to see Sita cry. He tried to console her by saying, "Do not cry, mother! Lord Rama will surely rescue you from Lanka. I have come here to ensure that you are safe. I shall go at once and inform Rama of your well-being. Once he hears the news from me, he will soon descend on Lanka with a mighty army of monkeys and bears. Please do not lose hope and give me, O mother, something of yours that I can show Rama to make him believe that I have met his beloved, Sita." said Hanuman.

Sita took out her hairpin, which Rama had gifted to her and giving it to Hanuman said, "Please give this to my lord and inform him that I am waiting for him with bated breath."

Hanuman is Captured

Hanuman decided to do something before leaving to instill fear among the demons and assure Sita of Rama's strength.

So he began to grow in size and started destroying the beautiful garden. He took a gigantic leap and landed on a jewel studded tree nearby, and started breaking its fruit laden branches. Next, he stomped his feet on the crystal pond allowing water to run out. Trees fell cracking to the ground, bowers collapsed, tanks and hillocks were destroyed.

The demonesses guarding the Ashoka Vatika fled in fear and reported the happenings to Ravana. Filled with rage, he ordered his soldiers to go at once and kill the monster-monkey. A strong force, armed with maces, spears and other mighty weapons set off to execute the king's commands. Demon warriors were amazed to see a vanara seated on the garden gate, who at their approach grew bigger in size. The warriors were no match to Hanuman, who with his mace struck them down, one by one.

Thus when the demon warriors failed to catch Hanuman, Ravana ordered his son Indrajit to catch the vanara. At the sight of Indrajit, Hanuman roared and increased his stature still further. The demon warrior aimed deadly arrows at Hanuman. No matter how often he was wounded, Hanuman didn't lose strength. Indrajit then aimed Brahmastra, the weapon of Brahma, at Hanuman. The weapon never missed its target, so Hanuman lay bound and helpless.

Lanka on Fire

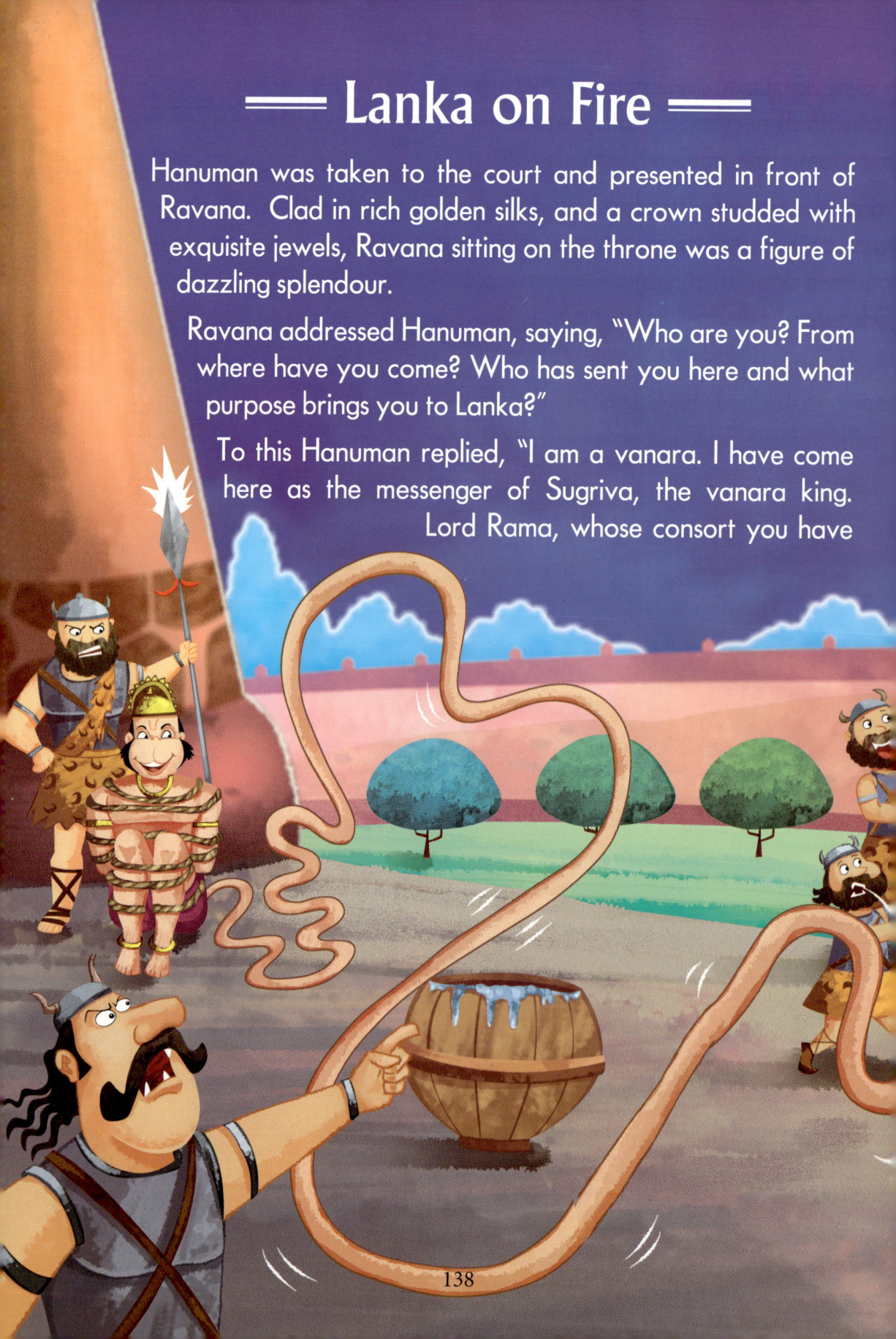

Hanuman was taken to the court and presented in front of Ravana. Clad in rich golden silks, and a crown studded with exquisite jewels, Ravana sitting on the throne was a figure of dazzling splendour.

Ravana addressed Hanuman, saying, "Who are you? From where have you come? Who has sent you here and what purpose brings you to Lanka?"

To this Hanuman replied, "I am a vanara. I have come here as the messenger of Sugriva, the vanara king. Lord Rama, whose consort you have abducted, is a dear friend of Sugriva. O lord of demons, what you have done is a cowardly act! Restore Sita to the prince and seek his forgiveness. Remember that death has come to you in the form of Sita."

When the demon king heard these words, his eyes grew red with anger, and he ordered that Hanuman should be killed. At this moment, Ravana's younger brother Vibhishana intervened, and said, "O king, don't forget that he is a messenger! The law prohibits a king to kill an envoy."

To this Ravana agreed and said, "Very well. A monkey's most cherished possession is his tail. Set his tail on fire and turn him out!"

Following the orders of Ravana the demons caught Hanuman, who was still tied with ropes, and dragged him out of the court. Next, they wrapped up his tail in rags. However, Hanuman gave them a hard time! His tail grew in size, and as it grew, they brought more and more old rags to wrap it. At last tired, they soaked the whole tail in oil and set it ablaze like a huge flaming torch. Thus bound by ropes and with tail ablaze, Hanuman was taken through the streets of Lanka.

Suddenly, Hanuman reduced himself in size and the ropes that bound him fell off. Coming back to his normal size, with a roar, he jumped into the air. With his tail blazing, Hanuman jumped from roof to roof, setting fire to them. Trees, mansions, houses, all were up in flames. Terrorized, demons ran hither and thither. Soon a strong breeze began to blow and the whole city was on fire.

Hanuman burnt the entire Lanka except the Ashoka Vatika. Before taking the final leap and starting his journey towards the sea, he took one last look at the golden city of Lanka, which was no longer golden!

Good Tidings Conveyed

The waiting vanaras were joyous at the sight of Hanuman.

Hanuman informed them about all that had happened in Lanka. After narrating the story, he said, "Shall we go straight to Lanka, destroy Ravana, bring Sita back and restore her to Rama?"

To this, old and wise Jambavan suggested, "No, it is not right. We should tell everything to Rama and Lakshmana and then do what they desire."

With this resolve, Hanuman and Angada, along with the vanaras, marched to Kishkindha, where Rama and Lakshmana were waiting for them.

With folded hands, Hanuman said to Rama, "I met Sita. She is kept as a prisoner in Ashoka Vatika. She passes her days thinking about you. She asked me to give you this." With these words, he handed the hair pin that Sita had given to Rama.

As Rama looked at the hair pin, his heart filled with sorrow. Choked with emotion, Rama said, "O heroic son of Vayu, blessed are you who have seen Sita. I too see her now before me. You have, indeed, brought her to me!"

Vanara King Sugriva tried to console grief-stricken Rama, saying, "Lay aside your grief, my Lord. My warriors are awaiting your command. Let us waste no more time and start our journey to Lanka!"

Sugriva reassured Rama, and inspired him to action. Thus, under the star of triumph, Uttara Phalguni, the army started towards the southern sea. When the army reached Mahendra Mountain, Rama climbed the peak, and looking at the vast sea in front of them, said, "This poses a big challenge in front of us. Let us camp in the forest until we decide on how to cross the massive sea."

Vibhishana Meets Rama

The next day, seated on Mahendra Mountain, Rama watched the dancing waves of the sea. Lanka looked like a tiny speck from this vast distance. He was in deep reverie, which was broken by Sugriva, who came accompanied by Vibhishana, the younger brother of Ravana.

With folded hands, Vibhishana said to Rama, "Oh, Lord! I am Vibhishana, the brother Ravana, who killed Jatayu and carried off

Sita by force. In vain I tried to counsel him to restore Sita back to you and seek your forgiveness. All that I received in return was disdain and humiliation. Hence, I stand here before you, renouncing my kingdom. I seek service and sanctuary at your feet."

Sugriva, who mistrusted the good faith of the demon king's brother, said to Rama, "Whatever Vibhishana may say, we cannot forget that he is the brother of our foe. How can we trust him? This could be some trick of Ravana. If we admit him into our camp, he may betray us at the first opportunity and return to his own people. It is best to deny him the favour he is asking for."

Rama, the epitome of dharma, responded, "If a man comes as a friend, how can I reject him? It is against my dharma. It does not matter even if I suffer as a result of this. Even if Ravana himself comes to me for sanctuary, I would accept him without hesitation. How then can I reject his brother who has done me no wrong?"

With these words, Rama embraced Vibhishana and accepted him. Vibhishana pledged undying friendship to Rama, whereas Rama ensured him that he would slay Ravana and make Vibhishana king of Lanka.

Crossing the Sea

The next morning, Sugriva, Vibhishana and Lakshmana, along with Rama, deliberated on how to cross the massive obstacle ahead of them, in the form of the great sea. Vibhishana suggested to Rama, "Why don't you start by offering prayers to the Sea God?"

Rama accepted the advice and started by sitting on the seashore, offering prayers to the Sea God, requesting him to grant a passage across. For three days he prayed. Answering his prayers, shining like the rising sun behind Mount Meru, the Sea God appeared before Rama.

With folded hands, he said, "O Lord Rama! I am subject to the laws of nature like the earth, air, space, light, and all constituents of the universe. How can I depart from my nature, which is to be vast, deep, and impassable? However, you may make a bridge to cross the sea. I will make a passage for your bridge. Nala, one of your generals, son of divine architect Vishwakarma, has the ability to build this path. This is the only way I can help you. May victory be yours!" With these words, the Sea God disappeared.

Thus the building of the bridge began. Infused with enthusiasm, the vanaras went to the mountains and forests to bring rocks and boulders to the shore. Hanuman chanted the divine mantra over each rock and boulder.

The work of building the bridge went on at great speed. Nala stood and supervised the work. The bridge thus constructed in five days was a hundred yojana long and ten yojana wide. The new path shone across the sea like the milky way in the sky. The vanaras shouted in exultation on their success, and the gods and rishis in heaven blessed them on their success.

Rama carried by Hanuman on his shoulders, and Lakshmana carried by Angada, set out to cross the bridge. Sugriva and the entire vanara army followed them. Thus Rama's army crossed the great sea.

The Battle Begins

At night, Rama's army settled at Mount Suvela to rest and plan for the war strategy ahead.

The next morning, they arranged forces to meet Ravana's massive army and each commander was assigned his task. Nila was to meet Prahasta at the eastern gate. Angada was to meet Mahaparsva and Mahodara at the southern entrance. At the western entrance Hanuman was to encounter Indrajit, the son of Ravana. Thus, the vanara army surrounded Lanka from all sides.

In a final attempt, Rama sent Angada to persuade Ravana to surrender without the war.

Angada went to Ravana and said, "I, Angada, son of Vali, have come here as Rama's messenger. Rama, son of Dasharatha, waits at the gates of your fortress, ready for battle. O king of demons, your end is approaching. Restore Sita to her lord and beg for forgiveness. If you are unwilling to surrender, then bid farewell to all your dear possessions in Lanka and prepare for death."

Hearing these words, Ravana's rage flared up like a flame. "Seize him, kill him! The villain!" he shouted.

At once, two demons caught hold of Angada. The next moment, Angada rose in the sky carrying those two demons on either side of him and then flinging them down. As soon as Angada returned and narrated the incident to him, Rama issued orders to the army to begin the assault on Lanka.

Serpent Darts

Following the orders of Rama, the vanara army rushed to the city of Lanka, shouting, "Victory to the vanara king! Victory to Rama and Lakshmana! Crush the demons."

The demon king Ravana sent forth a huge demon army with a command to slay all the vanaras at once. The vanaras used boulders and trees to oppose the demons. Thousands fell dead on either side. The battlefield was covered with blood and mutilated bodies.

Besides this gruesome engagement, there were many duels between individual warriors. Angada attacked Indrajit, slew his horses and charioteer and smashed the chariot. The vanaras admired the skill and strength of their prince and shouted with joy.

The battle raged throughout the day. Panic-stricken with his impending defeat, Indrajit used his magical powers. The next moment, he became invisible and shot serpent darts at Rama and Lakshmana. Bound by slimy serpents, Rama and Lakshmana lost consciousness and fell on to the ground.

Seeing Rama and Lakshmana in this state, the vanara warriors, wounded and downcast, concluded that all was over. At this moment Sushena, Sugriva's uncle suggested, "There are miracle herbs on Chandra and Drona mountains that can heal the wounds of the princes and restore them to health. Send Hanuman to fetch these herbs."

Hanuman was about to set out on this task, when a miracle happened. The great bird Garuda, the vehicle of Lord Vishnu, appeared. On arrival of Garuda, the serpent darts that covered Rama and Lakshmana disappeared instantaneously. Next, Garuda gently stroked Rama and Lakshmana and restored them back to health.

On gaining consciousness, when Rama asked, "Who are you, my benefactor?" Garuda replied, "I am Garuda, your old friend. I have broken the serpent spell cast by Indrajit. May victory be yours!" Saying this, the bird flew away.

Infused with enthusiasm on seeing the princes back to health, the vanaras resumed the battle and attacked Ravana's fortress.

When the news of Rama and Lakshmana being alive reached Ravana, he was filled with anger. After long deliberation, he called his generals and said, "The time has come when we should wake up Kumbhakarna. My younger brother, Kumbhakarna is needed here at my side."

The Giant is Roused

Kumbhakarna, Ravana's younger brother, was huge in size. Due to a curse, he slept for six months in a year and remained awake for the remaining six months.

Following Ravana's order, his ministers accompanied with servants went to Kumbhakarna's palace. They were well aware that as soon as he would open his eyes, he would be hungry. Therefore, they prepared and piled up mountains of food for him. Then they started beating drums and blowing conches and trumpets. The noise that they made filled the sky and frightened all the birds away, but Kumbhakarna in his sleep heard nothing! The demon then started pushing and shaking his huge body.

At last his eyes opened. The next moment, he brushed everyone aside and began to eat and drink.

Once he was satisfied, then Ravana's minister Yupaksha said, "My Lord, we stand in grave danger. Lanka is surrounded by vanaras led by Rama and Lakshmana. Lord Ravana desires your aid."

158

Kumbhakarna went to meet Ravana in his palace. Rejoicing at the news of his younger brother waking up from deep slumber, Ravana embraced him and said, "I know your love for me. I seek your help in this battle against Rama. Go at once and annihilate these enemies and save Lanka!"

Kumbhakarna, armed with his great spear, headed towards the battlefield. Seeing his huge form, the vanaras were frightened and started fleeing in all directions. No one could face Kumbhakarna. He began to kill and devour the vanaras. None of the vanara chiefs could hold him.

Lakshmana aimed his arrows at Kumbhakarna, but couldn't stop him. Rama was aware that ordinary arrows would be useless against such a huge demon. After some thought, he decided to use the magical weapons given to him by Sage Vishwamitra.

Thus, Rama invoked Vayu's weapon and severed Kumbhakarna's right arm. Then invoking Indra's arrow, he aimed at his left arm. However, Kumbhakarna still remained unperturbed. At last, Rama aimed a deadly arrow at Kumbhakarna's head and sliced it off! The severed head rose up into the sky, fell on the highest hill in Lanka and burst into flames.

Sanjeevani Booti

When the news of Kumbhakarna's death reached Ravana, he cried in grief and anger, "Ah mighty warrior! How could you go to Yama's world leaving me behind? It seems my end is near with Lanka losing all its mighty warriors!"

At this moment, Indrajit comforted his father, "Why should you worry when I am alive? I promise you that I will return with the heads of Rama and Lakshmana."

With these words, he proceeded to the battlefield with his army.

Indrajit swooped down on the vanara forces, killing and wounding thousands of them. They were helpless against his fury. His sky-shattering roars could make anyone run in fear. That was why, Indrajit was also known as Meghnada.

Lakshmana set out to kill Indrajit. A deadly battle ensued between the two. Indrajit invoked the Shakti a deadly weapon against Lakshmana. Lakshmana fell down on the ground unconscious.

Rama sat beside Lakshmana, grief-stricken. All the vanaras surrounded them. At this moment, Jambavan said to Hanuman, "The only cure for Shakti weapon is Sanjeevani Booti, which is a combination of herbs. It grows in Himalayas."

To this Hanuman immediately responded, "I will go there right away. But how will I find these herbs? Can you tell me what they look like?"

Jambavan answered, "In the Himalayas, they are the herbs which glow brightly. But hurry Hanuman! We need these herbs before sunrise tomorrow."

The next moment, Hanuman took a huge leap into the air and started his journey. Flying with the speed of wind, Hanuman soon reached the Himalayas. Standing amidst hundreds of herbs, Hanuman was confused, as he could not identify the right ones. As time was running out, Hanuman decided to carry the entire hill with him. The next moment, he lifted the Sanjeevani hill and started towards Lanka at the speed of lightning.

The vanaras awaited the arrival of Hanuman. As the Sanjeevani hill approached, the air was filled with soothing aroma of herbs, which revived Lakshmana. Rama embraced Lakshmana and thus the night of grief ended.

The Slaying of Indrajit

Once again battle resumed. Ravana sent Kumbha and Nikumbha, the sons of Kumbhakarna, to the battlefield, together with Yupaksha and other demon warriors.

After another terrible battle, Kumbha was slain by Sugriva and Nikumbha by Hanuman. Makaraksha, son of Khara, who opposed Rama, fell down to his fiery arrows. Many more mighty demons perished.

Seeing this, Indrajit decided to play a trick on Rama and his army. He rushed forward in his chariot and created an image of Sita through his magic. Catching the image of Sita by hair, Indrajit beheaded Sita in front of the entire army of the vanaras. Rama, Lakshmana along with the whole vanara army were grief-stricken. At this moment, Vibhishana intervened and consoled Rama by saying, "It is only a trick played by Indrajit! Ravana would never allow Sita to be killed."

Sugriva now ordered some of his trusted vanaras to enter Lanka and set fire to the city. They attacked the city and set fire to all the palaces and mansions in Lanka. The golden city was soon reduced to a mass of ashes. Amidst all this, Indrajit sat in a temple performing sacrifice. Completion of this sacrifice would bestow him powers which would make him invincible. Being one from the demon clan, Vibhishana was well aware of the moves of his clan. He said to Rama and Lakshmana, "If he completes the sacrifice, we cannot vanquish him. Lakshmana should, therefore, rush to obstruct the sacrifice."

Accepting his advice, Rama sent Lakshmana, accompanied by Hanuman and other vanaras, besides Vibhishana. They reached the spot where the sacrifice was in progress and Indrajit was about to offer oblations. Without wasting a moment, Lakshmana sent a shower of arrows, thus disrupting the sacrifice. Then a long and fierce battle ensued between Lakshmana and Indrajit, as they were well matched in strength and skill.

At last, Lakshmana invoked Indrastra, one of the most powerful weapons. Uttering the name of Rama, he discharged the fatal blow. Flying at the speed of light, Indrastra severed Indrajit's head off.

End of Ravana

When the news of Indrajit's death reached Ravana, and when he heard that Vibhishana helped Lakshmana in slaying Indrajit, his grief and anger knew no bounds. "Alas, my son! O peerless warrior! O hero! Vanquisher of the great Indra! Death has won after all? The world is now empty for me. Oh son, you have left me heart-broken and disconsolate. Nothing remains now but revenge and despair."

With these words, Ravana decided to avenge the death of his brother Kumbhakarna and his son Indrajit. With full faith in his prowess and in the efficacy of the boons he had, Ravana mounted his divine chariot drawn by eight horses and started towards the battlefield.

Ravana drove out to battle accompanied by his mighty warriors Virupaksha, Mahodara and Mahaparsva. The mighty demon warriors who followed Ravana were crushed down by a deadly flight of arrows. Ravana drove fast to the spot where Rama stood accompanied by Lakshmana and other warriors. Ravana showered a volley of deadly arrows at Rama. Rama easily tackled these arrows with his own and struck Ravana repeatedly, however failing to penetrate his armour.

Thus they fought, these supreme warriors, each bent on slaying the other and using increasingly potent weapons of secret power, while the gods in heaven looked on with marvel and admiration.

Rama aimed his arrows on the several heads of Ravana. The arrows didn't miss the target. Blood spurted out, but it didn't affect Ravana's strength. He stood there like a mountain! Neither of the warriors had met such an opponent before. On both sides admiration was mingled with wrath.

Then, suddenly, in the battlefield, a glorious chariot descended from heaven. Shining like sun, yoked to green horses and bearing a golden flag-staff, the chariot was sent by Indra for Rama.

Matali, Indra's charioteer, approached Rama with folded hands, and said, "Indra has sent this chariot to you for your victory. Here is also the great bow and the divine weapons belonging to Indra. O Lord, mount this chariot with me as a charioteer, and kill Ravana!"

Rama then ascended the chariot, causing the three worlds to shine with his splendour. Then once again ensued a great battle between the two warriors. Rama pierced every limb of Ravana with his arrows, and yet he did not fall! Ravana hurled Asurashastra at Rama, which turned into a ferocious beast and attacked him. Rama counter attacked with Agneyastra which burnt the beast into cinders.

Once again, Ravana aimed serpent arrows at Rama, which were countered by eagle arrows sent by Rama. The battle raged on between the two. Ravana took at an enormous spear and aimed at Rama. The spear met an array of arrows in the sky, sent by Rama. But to everyone's surprise, the arrows burnt off! Such intense was the power of the spear. Without wasting a moment, Rama took out the Shakti weapon given to him by Indra and hurled it in the air. In mid-air, the spear and Shakti collided and the spear broke into thousand pieces.

Every astra was met by another. In new and wonderful ways, the two warriors fought for a long time, while both armies watched the spectacle with both admiration and anxiety. Vibhishana, Hanuman, and Jambavan were anxious as Ravana seemed invincible. It was at this moment, Matali, the charioteer of Indra, said to Rama, "O the valiant one! O lord! It is time to use Brahmastra against him. His moment of death has arrived."

Rama, reminded thus by Matali, took hold of the blazing arrow, which was given to him by Sage Agastya and aimed it at Ravana. Rama knew the secret of Ravana's death. He knew that Ravana had the potion of immortality concentrated in his navel. So Rama aimed Brahmastra at Ravana's navel.

The moment Brahmastra struck his navel, Ravana's immortality was destroyed. The bow slipped from his hand; he fell down from the chariot and lay stretched on the battlefield.

Everyone rejoiced at the death of Ravana. The gods blew trumpets. Rama and his chariot were covered with flowers showered from heaven. Lakshmana, Vibhishana, Jambavan and other warriors surrounded Rama, in joy and adoration. The battlefield resounded with beating of drums and loud chanting of 'Jai Shri Rama' by the vanara army.

When the first flush of triumph was over and Vibhishana looked at the body of his brother, he was filled with sorrow. He burst into lamentations. "O great warrior!" he cried. "O scholar learned in all shastras! O valiant and famous king of kings! The worst I feared has happened now! You reaped what you sowed and you lie on the bare ground, O once mighty ruler of the demons!"

To Vibhishana thus lamenting, Rama said, "Ravana fought like a true warrior and fell fighting like a hero! Death has washed his sins. It calls for no mourning. Ravana has entered heaven."

Thus clearing all doubts from Vibhishana's mind, Rama bade him to perform the last rites of his departed brother.

The Test of Fire

Vibhishana was crowned as the king of Lanka in a magnificent ceremony. Vibhishana, having gained the great kingdom bestowed on him by Rama, was not only delighted but also grateful to him. After consoling his people, Vibhishana then sought the presence of Rama.

At this moment Rama said to Hanuman, "O Hanuman, the master of monkeys! With the king's permission, enter Lanka and inform Sita about our welfare and Ravana's death in the battle. After giving her this news, you ought to return here with her message."

As ordered, Hanuman accordingly took permission from Vibhishana and went to Ashoka Vatika to convey the news to Sita. On hearing, Hanuman's words, Sita's joy was beyond words. Unable to convey her happiness in words, she remained silent.

"Why, mother," asked Hanuman, "why are you silent?"

"What is there to say, my son?" she answered. "How can I repay my debt to you? Your wisdom, your valour, your prowess, your patience, your humility are all your own. None in the world can equal you." As she said these words, her eyes filled with tears of gratitude and affection.

Troubled at the thought of how much Sita had suffered, Hanuman grew angry. Looking at the demonesses who had guarded Sita, he said to her, "I wish to slay these cruel women who troubled you. Do give me permission!" "No, my son," Sita answered. "Who in the world is blameless? It is the nature of noble souls to be compassionate towards all sinners as well as good people. These demonesses carried out the orders of their master. How are they to blame? Their king is dead and has paid for his crime. It is unjust to punish these demonesses now."

These words thus said by Sita are treasured like nectar by generations of pious men.

"What message am I to carry to Rama?" Hanuman asked Sita.

"I am eager to be in his presence," she answered. "That is all."

Hanuman returned to Rama and gave a detailed account of his visit. Rama turned to Vibhishana and said, "Ask Sita to bathe and bedeck herself, and then bring her here."

When Vibhishana conveyed this message to Sita in Ashoka Vatika, she said, "I would rather go as I am." To this Vibhishana said, "The prince's orders should be obeyed." So after a bath, bedecked with jewels and seated in palanquin, Sita was carried to meet Rama.

Rama was filled with both joy and indignation on Sita's arrival.

Alighting from the palanquin, with downcast eyes, Sita proceeded towards Rama. "Oh, Lord," she sobbed, unable to speak anymore. Sita expected to hear words of comfort and love from Rama. She waited, but didn't hear a word from him. Then she looked up and was shocked to see that Rama had turned his face away from her.

"My Lord, why are you looking away from me?" asked Sita.

"I have slain the enemy," said Rama. "I have rescued you. I have done my duty as a kshatriya. My vow is now fulfilled."

Incomprehensible and completely unexpected were these words which were uttered by Rama. His face darkened, and then he spoke even harsher words, "It was not for mere attachment to you that I waged this war. It was my duty as a kshatriya! I waged this war to get rid of evil. I fought this war to make this earth free from the atrocities of a demon. It gives me no joy now to get you back, as doubt envelops you like a dark cloud of smoke. How can a kshatriya take back his wife who has lived so long in a stranger's house?"

Hearing these words, Sita's heart filled with sorrow. Her eyes flashed fire! Looking at Rama, she said, "You have spoken unworthy words! My heart breaks to learn that you don't trust me. Does my lord forget my lineage? Was it my fault that the wicked demon seized me by force and imprisoned me? My devotion, my chastity, all have been ignored by you. However, if that's how you look upon me, then there is only one course open to me."

Sita then spoke to Lakshmana, "O Lakshmana! Kindle a fire. I no longer wish to live burdened with false accusations. I will enter the fire to embrace the only course left for a wife abandoned by a husband amidst an assembly of men."

Lakshmana, who had been watching Rama's behaviour in dismay and indignation, turned to look at Rama's face seeking his orders, but Rama did not say 'No' to Sita's request nor indicated any sign of softening.

With eyes filled with tears, Lakshmana built the pyre and lit the fire. Everyone gasped in horror as Sita stepped towards the fire and offered prayers, "O gods, I bow before you. Oh Agni, you know that I am pure. My mind has never strayed from the thought of Rama. Give me solace in your flames forever."

With these words she walked into the flames. The flames rose higher and higher, and reached up to the sky. Sita sitting in the centre of the pyre was soon hidden among the bright red flames. And then wonder of wonders happened! From the flames appeared Agni God, who said to Rama, "Sita is the epitome of purity! She is as pure as panchatattva. Take her back!"

With these words, he lifted Sita and brought her to Rama's side. Sita looked beautiful with a glow on her face. In her beautiful ornaments and splendid clothes she shone like the morning sun.

Rama held Sita's hand and said, "I knew that you were as pure as the holy water of River Ganga. This ordeal was to satisfy the people who would have thought that blinded by love Rama broke the rule of well-brought-up men. You are my beloved and not even for a second I doubted your purity. I hope you understand this and forgive me."

Sita smiled in affirmation and the gods showered flowers on them from heaven.

Rama and Sita, now reunited, accompanied by Lakshmana and their vanara friends ascended the Pushpaka Vimana which carried them swiftly to Ayodhya. Hanuman flew ahead of them to convey the news of Rama's return to Bharata.

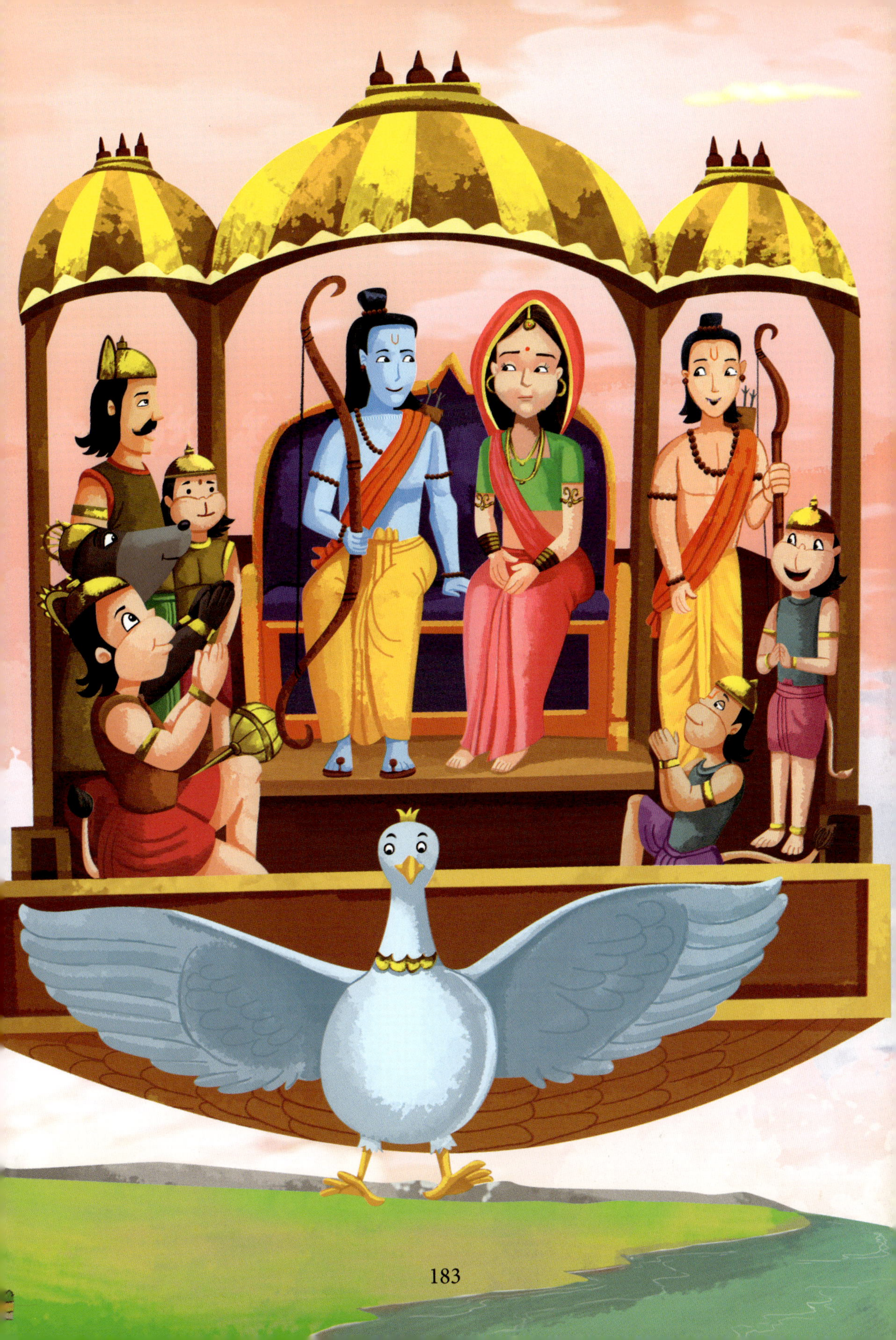

Rama, the King of Ayodhya

Back in Ayodhya, Bharata prepared for the home coming of his elder brother with unimaginable grandeur. For fourteen years, Bharata had waited eagerly for his brother to return. During these long years when

Rama was in exile, Bharata had lived like a hermit in a small cottage. As soon as the Pushpaka Vimana landed, Bharata rushed to touch Rama's feet. Rama, Lakshmana and Sita met their mothers, Kaushalya, Sumitra and Kaikeyi, who was ashamed of her deeds.

The city of Ayodhya danced in joy. It is believed that Rama returned to Ayodhya on the night of Amavasya, when there was no moonlight. People of Ayodhya lit their homes and the path on which Rama was to pass, with diyas. Since then, the day of Lord Rama's return to Ayodhya is celebrated every year as Deepavali, the festival of lights.

Sage Vashishtha ordered arrangements for Rama's coronation to be made. Rama was anointed as the king of Ayodhya. The city of Ayodhya rejoiced.

In the years that followed, Ayodhya prospered under the reign of Rama. People were happy and healthy, as Rama was a just and brave king.

The laws in the land of Rama were equal for all. There was no discrimination of rich and poor. There were no thieves, robbers or beggars in the kingdom. People never locked their houses. The rule of Rama, known as 'Rama Rajya', was based on the foundation of dharma and truth. Vedas were its guiding principles.

Birth of Luv and Kush

While Rama adorned the throne of Ayodhya, all the great sages came to visit him. They praised him, especially as he had slain the sons of Ravana, mightier than Ravana himself, and had liberated men and gods from fear.

The vanaras stayed in the kingdom of Ayodhya for more than a month, feasting on honey, fruits and roots. When the time came for them to go back, Rama embraced every one with affection and gave them gifts. But Hanuman bowed and begged for the boon that he might ever be devoted to Rama alone, and that he might live on earth as long as the story of the deeds of Rama was told amongst men. Rama granted the boon and took a jewelled chain from his own neck and put it upon Hanuman.

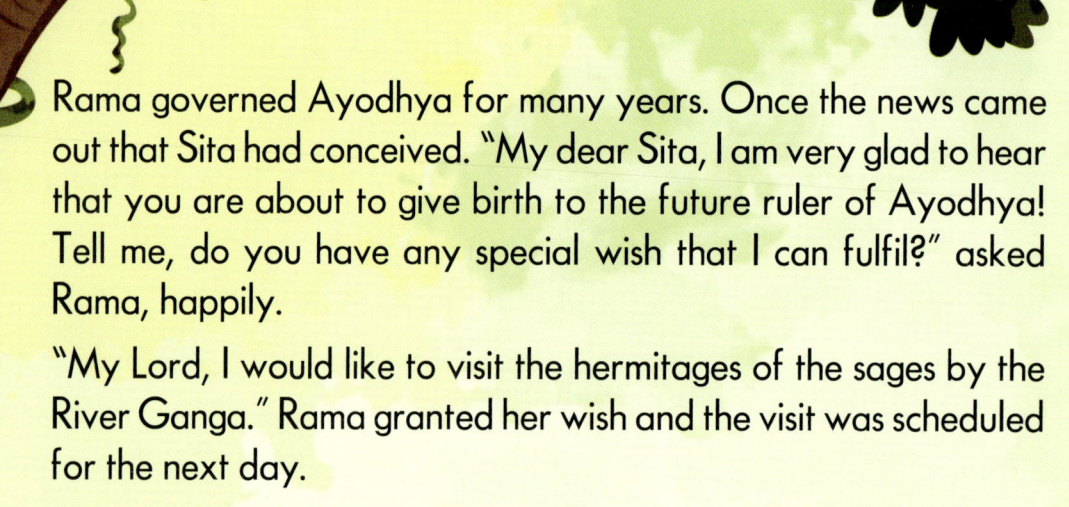

Rama governed Ayodhya for many years. Once the news came out that Sita had conceived. "My dear Sita, I am very glad to hear that you are about to give birth to the future ruler of Ayodhya! Tell me, do you have any special wish that I can fulfil?" asked Rama, happily.

"My Lord, I would like to visit the hermitages of the sages by the River Ganga." Rama granted her wish and the visit was scheduled for the next day.

That very night, Rama came to know from his ministers that his subjects were happy that he killed Ravana. But, they were not pleased that he brought back Sita with him, as she had stayed for long in the house of a different person other than her husband.

Hearing this, Rama was very distressed. He had full faith in his wife, but being an ideal king, he could not ignore his subjects too. And so, he decided to keep his subjects happy.

"O God! You are compelling me to do injustice to my Sita. But alas! I am bound by my duty," he lamented. Then very sadly, he told Lakshmana to go and leave Sita in the jungle.

Lakshmana thus left Sita in the hermitage of Valmiki and returned to Ayodhya.

Dwelling in the hermitage of Valmiki, Sita gave birth to two sons. They were named Kush and Luv. They grew up in the hermitage and Valmiki trained them with great wisdom. He wrote the story of Rama in shlokas and taught it to them.

Sita Enters the Earth

When Rama came to know that Luv and Kush were his sons and that Sita was living in the hermitage of Valmiki, he sent a message to the sage. Rama asked if Sita would like to return to Ayodhya.

Valmiki accompanied Sita to Ayodhya and then again something terrible happened. Rama again asked Sita to prove her faithfulness towards him.

"Lord, you have mistrusted me yet again! It is too much for me to bear!" said Sita, tearfully.

With this Sita prayed to Vasundhara (Mother Earth) to accept her, since she was ever faithful to Rama. A heavenly throne rose up from within the earth, borne on the heads of mighty nagas decked in shining jewels. Mother Earth stretched out her arms and embraced Sita, placing her on the throne. The throne sank down again.

Last Days of Rama

Rama became very sad with Sita's disappearance inside the earth before his very eyes. The whole world seemed empty without her. He made a golden statue of Sita to participate with him in the performance of sacred rites. Many years passed like this.

Then Kaushalya and Kaikeyi died. Bharata reigned in Kekaya, and Shatrughna was king of Madhu, while the sons of Lakshmana founded kingdoms of their own. One day, there came a yogi who called himself Kaal or Time. He told Rama that he was the avatar or incarnation of Lord Vishnu and that he had accomplished his goal by killing Ravana and reigning on earth for many years. He advised Rama that the time had come for his return to heaven. Rama accepted his advice, and along with his brothers and several demons and vanaras, he went to River Sarayu, from where they all went to heaven.

And thus ended Ramayana with the renunciation of worldly life by Rama.

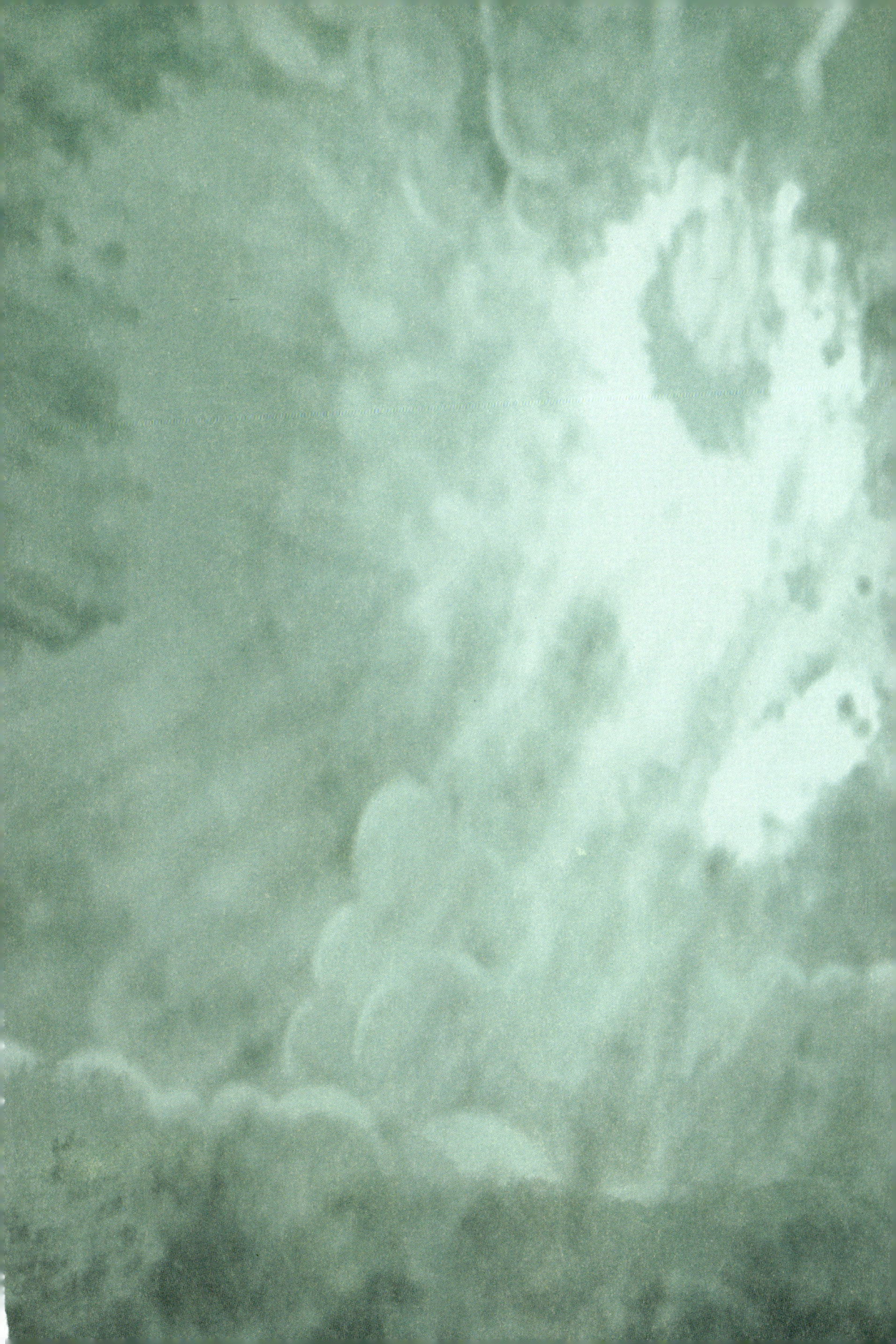